"A harrowing, deeply personal manifesto on our responsibility to the poor. Humane, grace-filled, and literally reverberating with prophetic vigor, *Make Poverty Personal* deserves to be read by a wide and grateful audience."

—**Alan Hirsch**, author of *The Forgotten Ways*

"Ash Barker and the UNOH revolution invite us to hear, smell, and touch Jesus in his most distressing disguises: in the slums, with the poor, in the most abandoned places of empire in which we find ourselves."

—**Shane Claiborne**, *The Simple Way*, Philadelphia

"An invitation to unlearn so much of conventional church faith and to learn afresh about God's good news for the world. There is a clarity that will let many readers come to grips, perhaps for the first time, with the revolutionary, subversive intention of the Bible."

—**Walter Brueggemann**, Columbia Theological Seminary

"Personal, passionate, authentic, challenging, engaging, relevant. This is no programmatic or utopian vision for ending poverty and injustice in our deeply wounded world. Instead, this is powerful testimony, rooted in the biblical story, in costly discipleship, and in risk-taking involvement to follow Jesus, the servant of God to the poor."

—**Charles Ringma**, professor emeritus, Regent College, Vancouver, Canada

"Here is a searing biblical call to end poverty, coming not from the safety of the snug office of an economist, an academic or a theologian, but from deep inside the bowels of the largest slum in Thailand. *Make Poverty Personal* is a discomforting, energizing, and ultimately hopeful read."

—**Michael Frost**, coauthor of *The Shaping of Things to Come*

Also by Ash Barker:

Making Connections
Collective Witness
Finding Life: Reflections from a Bangkok Slum
Surrender All: A Call to Sub-merge with Christ

Emergent Village resources for communities of faith

An Emergent Manifesto of Hope
edited by Doug Pagitt and Tony Jones

Organic Community
Joseph R. Myers

Signs of Emergence
Kester Brewin

Justice in the Burbs
Will and Lisa Samson

Intuitive Leadership
Tim Keel

The Great Emergence
Phyllis Tickle

www.emersionbooks.com

MAKE POVERTY PERSONAL

Taking the Poor as Seriously as the Bible Does

Ash Barker

BakerBooks

a division of Baker Publishing Group
Grand Rapids, Michigan

© 2009 by Ash Barker

Published by Baker Books
a division of Baker Publishing Group
P.O. Box 6287, Grand Rapids, MI 49516-6287
www.bakerbooks.com

First published 2006
by Urban Neighbours of Hope
PO Box 89
Springvale Vic 3171
Australia

Printed in the United States of America

Library of Congress Cataloging-in-Publication Data
Barker, Ash.
    Make poverty personal : taking the poor as seriously as the Bible does / Ash
Barker.
      p.   cm.
    Includes bibliographical references (p.   ).
    ISBN 978-0-8010-7189-8 (pbk.)
    1. Poverty—Religious aspects—Christianity. 2. Poverty—Biblical teaching.
3. Church work with the poor. I. Title.
BV4647.P6B37 2009
261.8′325—dc22   2008031186

ēmersion is a partnership between Baker Books and Emergent Village, a growing, generative friendship among missional Christians seeking to love our world in the Spirit of Jesus Christ. The ēmersion line is intended for professional and lay leaders like you who are meeting the challenges of a changing culture with vision and hope for the future. These books will encourage you and your community to live into God's kingdom here and now.

Ash Barker leads us on an important journey that is both personal and historical. **Make Poverty Personal** reminds us of the difference between personal and private. This book will inspire communities to put at the forefront of their efforts caring for the poor in ways that come from our normal, everyday lives. This call is to a real-life engagement with those who are in need not only for their benefit, but for ours as well.

Additionally, this book calls us to re-walk, with our words and our lives, the path of caring for the poor—a path walked by those of faith throughout history. Ash does not leave us simply with a call for better intentions, but a way forward for healthy engagement in our world.

This book serves communities of faith today as the kind of encouragement the Apostle Paul received in the early days of the church when he was called to "remember the poor," which was the very thing he was eager to do (Gal. 2:10). This is a book that calls some to a new vision, and others to recommit to the path they have already been walking.

Emergent Village resources for communities of faith

Contents

Foreword   9

Preface   13

Introduction   15

1 Beyond Excuses: Moses, the Exodus, and Courage to Face the Nature of Poverty   28

2 Hebrew Laws and "Always Having" Poverty   50

3 Hebrew Poetry and the Awesome Truth   64

4 Prophetic Ministry—Radical Hope from the Margins   83

5 The Gospels and Messianic Transformations   112

6 The Early Church: Standing Against Poverty Together   136

7 Epistles: Letters from Jail and Other Tough Places of Discipleship   158

8 Apocalypse Now: Last Things and the Things That Last   179

Final Challenge: Will We Make Poverty Personal?   194

Bibliography   201

Foreword

Oh yes, God is moving in the world.

Across the globe there are signs of a church that is closer to the poor and further from the drums of nationalism and war. We can see an emerging church that looks more like Jesus than the evangelicalism with which many of us grew up. Ash Barker and the Urban Neighbors of Hope (UNOH) revolution invite us to hear, smell, and touch Jesus in his most distressing disguises: in the slums, with the poor, in the most abandoned places of the empire in which we find ourselves. In a world that has found it hard to hear the words of Christian preachers because of the noise and contradictions of their lifestyles, Ash Barker is one of those folks whose life reflects the things he believes. Ash's stories point us towards a new kind of Christianity for which the world longs—a Christianity that looks like Jesus, and whose gospel is actually good news to the poor.

I grew up in a Christianity that tried to scare the hell out of us, literally. It had little hope to offer this world and just tried to pacify folks with the promise that there is life after death . . . while most of us were really asking, "Is there life before death?"

I remember as a child hearing all the hellfire and damnation sermons. We had a theater group perform a play called "Heaven's Gates and Hell's Flames." In this play, actors presented scenes of folks being ripped away from loved ones, only to be sent to the fiery pits of hell, where there is weeping and gnashing of teeth. We all went forward to repent of all the evil things we had done over our first decade of life, paralyzed by the fear of being "left behind." Since those days, I have grown to love the kind of Christianity about which Ash writes—a Christianity that is about loving people out of the hells of this world, not just trying to scare them into heaven.

Have you ever noticed that Jesus didn't spend much time on hell? In fact, there are really only a couple of times he speaks of weeping and gnashing of teeth, of hell and God's judgment, and both of them are about "making poverty personal." Both of them have to do with the walls we create between ourselves and our suffering neighbors. One is Matthew 25, where the sheep and the goats are separated; the goats, who did not care for the poor, hungry, homeless, and imprisoned, are sent off to endure an agony akin to that experienced by the ones they neglected on this earth.

Then there is Jesus's parable of the rich man and Lazarus. In this parable, we hear of a wealthy man who builds a gap between himself and the poor man, a gap that becomes an unbridgeable chasm not only from Lazarus, but also from God. He is no doubt a religious man (he calls out for "Father" Abraham and knows the prophets), and undoubtedly he made a name for himself on earth. Now, however, he is a nameless rich man begging the beggar for a drop of water. Lazarus, on the other hand, who lived a nameless life in the shadows of misery, is seated next to God and is given a name. Lazarus is the only person named in Jesus's parables; his name means "the one God rescues."

God is in the business of rescuing people from the hells they experience on earth, and God is asking us to love people out of those hells. God is asking us to taste the salt in the tears of the broken, to hunger for justice with the starving masses of our world, to groan with all of creation in the birth pains of the kingdom of God. God is asking us to make poverty personal.

I am convinced that the tragedy in the church is not that rich folks don't care about poor folks, but that rich folks don't *know* poor folks. Amid all the campaigns, issues, slogans, and political agendas, perhaps the deepest hunger in the world is: "Make Poverty Personal." The prophet Amos cries out that if our faith does not bring justice flowing like a river, then we should cease the clamor of all of our religious festivals and gatherings and songs, for they are noise in God's ears (Amos 5:21–24). And lest we let the liberals off the hook, I've met plenty of progressive "social justice" types who have shown that it is very easy to live a life of socially-conscious comfort that is compartmentalized and detached from any true relationships with the poor.

Mother Teresa once said, "It is very fashionable to talk about the poor . . . unfortunately it is not as fashionable to talk to the poor." Ash's message is simple—meet Christ in the least of these. Ash's vision is big—it is the vision of the kingdom of God coming on earth. But he realizes that the revolution begins inside each of us; as Christ said, the "kingdom is within you." The vision for changing the world must begin small, like a mustard seed. After all, when a reporter asked Mother Teresa how she had managed to pick up 50,000 folks from the streets of Calcutta, she said, "I began with one." Here is your invitation to begin with one.

As we enter these stories of God at work in the slums, it is like we are reading another chapter in the book of Acts—Acts 29. Ash and the folks conspiring with him are continuing to write the story of God's movement in the world. And they dare us to see ourselves as living epistles, people who can shout the gospel with our lives.

There's much work to do. The church is still a mess. As Augustine is said to have stated, "The church is a whore, but she's my mother." Or, as one of our pastors here in Philly said, "The church is like Noah's ark—it stinks sometimes, but if you get out, you'll drown." Ash's book is a reminder that there is new life emerging from the compost of Christendom. Every few hundred years it seems that Christianity faces an identity crisis. The fiery revolutions of God become institutionalized and stale, infected by power and triumphalism, suffocated by materialism, and begin to die. Then another remnant of Christ-followers goes to the deserts, to the slums, to the forsaken corners of our world to practice resurrection. Ash Barker is one of the prophetic voices in the wilderness calling people out of the centers of power and privilege to meet God on the margins. It is a call to re-imagine church—outside the walls, buildings, and meetings—as a body living out God's love across the globe. Through these pages we meet a creator who makes humanity from dirt, a Savior who enters the world as a baby refugee in the middle of Herod's genocide, and a Holy Spirit who continues to dwell in the "least of these."

There is so much noise and clutter in the Christian industrial complex, especially here in the West. Books line the shelves with advice on how to find our best life, how to live with purpose, and how to find God's blessing and the secret to prosperity. Here is a book that flies in the face of prosperity Christianity. Here is a book that reveals the true secret to fulfillment: if you really want to find your life then you should give it away. The best thing we can do with the blessings of God is to share them with the poor. That's not the message of the televangelists and prosperity preachers, but that is the gospel that rises from the ghettoes, from a homeless baby with no place to lay his head, from the slums of Bangkok and Galilee, from which people say "nothing good can come." Turn the page and get ready to meet a God with a special fondness for the badlands, a God whose kingdom is upside-down, a God who invites you to change the world with a love that does not conform.

Shane Claiborne
The Simple Way, Philadelphia, PA
Author of *The Irresistible Revolution*

Preface

God's heartbeat for the poor is finding new ways of expression. One indication of this is the book you have in your hands. Written in regular snatches from our slum home in Bangkok, its publication is nothing short of miraculous to me.

In late November 2005 I had completed a draft of this book. At that point, I had an energetic phone conversation with my good friend, Mick Pilbrow, in Canberra, Australia. We were talking about the "One Campaign" (in Australia it is called the "Make Poverty History" campaign), and we realized we had something to offer the then raging debate about ending poverty.

In a sudden whirl of efforts in Bangkok (me, crazily re-writing my draft), Canberra (editor, Geoff Alves), and Melbourne (designer Nick Wight and proofreaders Naomi Dekker, Stephen Barrington, Mike Lane, Dean Hurlston, and Russell Kilgour), this book was fast-tracked into print. It was first made available through our community's publishing arm, UNOH Publications, in March 2006. I am grateful to all who weaved their magic on this project.

In my native country, Australia, the response to that first edition was overwhelming. The book was short-listed for "Australian

Christian Book of the Year." It was then named "Best Christian Book Ever" in an internet poll by the Australian Christian web magazine. The book clearly seemed to make sense to all kinds of Christians. If God's heartbeat was for the poor, then God's people should step out and make poverty personal, too.

This edition would not be possible if not for the support of Mike Frost, Shane Claiborne, and Nick Wight. Their advocacy and solidarity was essential. I am so grateful for their support for this book and their friendship in life. I am also greatly appreciative of Bob Hosack and his team from Baker Books who believed this book should be made available to a much wider readership and had the patience and tenacity to see it through.

I especially want to thank my family. Having an absent-minded husband/father/son is not much fun at the best of times, and this was especially so around the first deadline for the Australian edition. They had to put up with my preoccupation on our first all-family holiday together in years as I fought with that first draft in Chang Mai. Their love, patience, and support of me in seeing dreams like this book come true fuels my life. I pray I can return the favor.

Finally, this book is dedicated to those gospel workers living out its key themes among the urban poor—both those who intentionally move into harm's way and those who have little choice. I pray this book will do our Savior proud, and will enable more gospel workers to take poverty personally and share the work load in our ready and waiting urban harvest fields.

Introduction

Opening Reflection: Saw's Poor Threads

Saw awoke with a sharp pain running through his stomach. Sitting bolt upright, he looked over at his fellow workers, still sleeping, lined up on mats in three rows. The sunlight started to break through the gaps in the rusty corrugated iron ceiling. Soon, one by one, each weary laborer would blink awake to a new day and it would begin again.

Saw sighed, envious of their rest, however fleeting it would be, for yesterday they had worked almost eighteen hours straight to complete a set of rugs ready for export. Little sleep, a little rice and sloppy curry, then long hours of weaving. He might have lost track of the time if he wasn't counting down the days until he would see his wife and two daughters and all his family and friends back in his village on the other side of the border. Just thirteen days to go.

But even this brief thought of his family couldn't bring a smile to Saw's face this morning. He felt as though a tiny knife had entered his intestines and was filleting him from the inside out. Another eighteen hours in front of the machine just didn't seem possible.

The night before a friend had conjured up a mixture of herbs and green liquid, but rather than helping, it had kept him awake.

"What can I do?" Saw mumbled to himself. If he stopped work, he would not be paid for any of his last month's work; and if he was not paid, his family would not be able to repay its debts back in the village. He couldn't let them all down now. Saw staggered out the back of the laborers' shed to the concrete squat toilet. He got dizzier as he peed and pooed out blood. Surveying the mess, Saw realized he just couldn't keep going.

"Surely someone cares about what's happening to us here," he lamented to the small gecko climbing above the door. "It's not just the craps—it's the whole way we're forced to live. Less than $30 a month for hundreds of weavings. They sell them in the West for thousands each. It makes the boss's family one of the richest in town. If I could just get a message out, surely somebody could do something? But what can an illegal migrant worker do?"

Just then a desperate idea came to him. "What if I were to weave a message, and pray that the boss doesn't see it but that others do? Maybe someone would stand with us." Saw knew it was a long shot, full of risk, but it was all he could think of in that blood-filled, agonizing moment. He knew he couldn't last thirteen more days. . . .

✝

John and Teresa were walking through a factory outlet that was having a closing-down sale. They had never seen such cheap floor rugs and wall hangings before. "What intricate and colorful weavings," Teresa exclaimed.

They needed a wall hanging for their brand-new home and, after seeing the TV ad late the night before, they drove out the next morning, anticipating a bargain.

"What about that one?" John said, hoping to get it over with so he could get to his friend's place to watch the soccer game.

"Won't match the olive curtains, love, but I just adore that one," said Teresa, pointing to a dark-green and maroon weaving hanging on the factory wall with a red sale sign saying, "Only $99." It had an odd pattern up close, but they pulled it down from the wall before someone else did.

"I'm not sure it goes that well on the wall after all," Teresa said. "It's not the right shade of green."

"What about on the floor of the kid's bedroom?" John asked.

They took the weaving to Jody's room, swept Barbie and her latest outfits out of the way, and whooshed the weaving down.

"Not bad. Not great, but it could protect the carpet a bit, and we can't return it," John said.

"It'll do for now, I guess," said Teresa.

Just then little Jody bounced in with a few friends.

"Wow, Mum! What a mat! It's great. Barbie just loves it, too!"

Jody looked at the mat, fiddling with her blonde curly locks, then asked, "But Mum, what does 'Please stand with me' mean?"

"What?"

"'Please stand with me.' You know, what it says on the mat?"

The Bible's Concern for the Poor

We live in a world where this story could be a real-life parable and not just a figment of my imagination to help frame our discussions. The Bible is like a precious weaving made by God through oppressed people. Yet, its cry for help is mostly ignored. The call is loud and obvious, but people are so distracted with other agendas that those who need to hear it most miss it.

A remarkable confession was made recently by Rick Warren. Warren is a well-known Christian minister and author of *The Purpose Driven Life*, which has sold more than 26 million copies. *Christianity Today* magazine reported Rick Warren's experience of poverty in Africa:

> "Around this time," Warren says, he was driven to re-examine scripture with "new eyes." What he found humbled him. "I found those 2,000 verses on the poor. How did I miss that? I went to Bible college, two seminaries, and I got a doctorate. How did I miss God's compassion for the poor? I was not seeing all the purposes

of God. The church is the body of Christ. The hands and feet have been amputated and we're just a big mouth, known more for what we're against." Warren found himself praying, "God, would you use me to re-attach the hands and the feet to the body of Christ, so that the whole church cares about the whole gospel in a whole new way—through the local church?"

Timothy C. Morgan, "Purpose Driven in Rwanda,"
Christianity Today, October 2005

What is remarkable is not that such a well-credentialed minister missed God's message and heart for the poor for so long—surely this is to be expected in a success-driven culture. Rather, what is remarkable is that Warren had the humility to publicly confess missing the Bible's concern and was prepared to do something about it. But if someone like Warren has missed the message, how many others are there who have missed it too?

Jim Wallis, from the Sojourners Community in Washington, is one Western Christian leader who hasn't missed the Bible's concern for the poor. In the 1970s he and a colleague actually went through the whole Bible with a pair of scissors and cut out every one of the 2,000 verses that related to poverty and injustice. His was a very hole-y Bible indeed! People in pews were aghast as this cut-and-paste Bible was held up. But, as he pointed out, this is what most Christians do with this most holy book.

Some might say that ending poverty is really the domain of activists, economists, and politicians. What does Christianity have to offer to help end poverty? It is time that Christians reconsider what the Bible has to say about poverty. Specifically, what are its concerns about the nature of poverty, and what does God require of us?

This book is the result of my search for answers to these questions as a Christian who lives in a large, urban slum in Bangkok and, before that, lived for ten years in one of Melbourne's poorest neighborhoods. Since April Fools' Day 2002, our life here as a family in Klong Toey has disoriented me and driven me back to want to know what God has to say about poverty here.

For example, what about little kids like May? The normally well-kept little girl with a cheeky grin suddenly started to lose weight and came to our Klong Toey preschool with matted and dirty hair. Our experienced Thai teachers knew that both of May's parents died of an HIV/AIDS-related illness and that she was looked after by her remarkable grandmother. But when they went to visit May at home—a shack that hangs precariously over a stinking, dirty creek, with an on-ramp of a freeway for its roof—even they were shocked. May's grandma, who had been caring for ten other grandchildren and some other children, had died suddenly in her sleep. As the children awoke to a new reality, the older kids had to take care of the younger ones. There were two teenagers who were working to support all eleven of them. If ever there was a time for solidarity, to stand with a family, it was now. Being available and being a presence was as important as any material help.

What hope is there for May and the thousands of kids like her without solidarity? Her physical, emotional, economic, and spiritual start has been stunted. Can she ever fulfill the dignity God intended for her? Or will this little five-year-old become fodder for the prostitution and go-go bar scene, like so many of our neighbors before her? We organized a family scholarship for May via the center, the staff began to visit regularly with food and support, and I "hit the books" and pleaded for God's intervention for May and the bigger picture of poverty.

What does God have to say in the Bible about poverty like this? While there are differences between life in Bible times and today—global banking, travel, and commerce, to name just a few—what I found was that God reveals the very nature of poverty and sews a thread of response throughout the Bible. As I took time most mornings to trace and reflect prayerfully on this thread, I better understood what our response to poverty can be if we take poverty as seriously and as personally as God does.

The Bible too often has been reduced to children's entertainment, rather than the greatest revealed response to poverty and injustice ever written. For when it comes to understanding and responding to poverty, the best book to read is still the Bible.

Taken collectively, its concerns show us how to respond to the suffering and tragedy that causes and leaves humans in poverty, both in Bible times and today. Yet this library of insights and pleas is rarely appreciated, and even more rarely acted upon. This can be attested to by the fact that 99 percent of Western church income is spent on itself.

If you take the thread of this message out of the Bible, the Bible will quickly unravel. God's special concern for the poor is developed as a stronger and stronger theme as the revelation of God's will becomes clearer. Will we read God's Word with eyes wide open? Will we allow Scripture to inspire and inform what we do with our lives? Will we hear the pleas from the Saws and Mays of the world?

Making Our Lives Count in a Fragile World

While few Christians know the Bible well enough to see its real answers to poverty, the world in which we live is becoming more aware of its precarious situation and the desperate need to take poverty seriously. If the people of our volatile world are to have a common future together, then poverty has to go. If you need a reminder of how fragile the world is, remember Boxing Day 2004. I was in a food court not far from my home in Klong Toey slum, my bleary eyes trying to focus on a Bono quote in a *Bangkok Post* article above the din of the lunchtime crowd.

"We have the cash. We have the medicines. We have the technologies. But do we have the will? Do we have the will to make poverty history?"

My mind was drifting, however. "One more church service and we're off on holidays." Although we had planned to go on holidays that day, Anji had managed to get $15 flights to Phuket for the next. My whole body seemed to ache to get off concrete and collapse into the sand and salt water. "I guess my will to end poverty will have to wait."

When I arrived home, our neighbors told us there had been some kind of storm in Phuket. It was a bad one. Apparently, there had been some flooding and windows broken. However, the BBC and Reuters websites reported deaths from an earthquake and a tsunami. Numbness overwhelmed me, and I soon fell asleep on our couch. Anji, of course, was in fast mode and chased up every lead as to what to do about our holiday. (They say opposites attract!) She booked a cheap guesthouse at Pattaya, near Bangkok, arranged to borrow a friend's car, and cancelled our hotel and flights. "So travelling tomorrow isn't convenient for you?" the Air-Asia receptionist asked Anji.

In our room at Pattaya the next day we saw our first full TV report. It felt like we were watching *Schindler's List*, as bodies of children were dragged from beaches and piled up next to each other. Within a week over 150,000 were reported dead, including around 6,000 people from around Phuket.

While I was reading Bono, one of the worst natural disasters in recent history had occurred.

Bono's question finally got my attention. Would the will to respond come? A strangely united world answered by pledging two billion dollars within a week. Ships, helicopters, and volunteers were mobilized to bring relief. Just as the tsunami tragedy affected rich and poor, celebrities and the anonymous, Muslim, Buddhist, Hindu, and Christian alike, so too did the responses flow from diverse people and groups around the world. Like me, the world knew it could have been any one of us.

For me the most harrowing accounts came from parents who lost their children. "Why them? Why not me?" they cried. When a little blond boy about my son Aiden's age survived on floating debris and was picked up by a villager and taken back to town, a deep sense of survivor guilt hit me, too. As I watched the latest news (and, for some relief, cricket from a South African cable channel), I had to reflect: "Why not our family? Why were we spared?"

My only conclusion was that no one deserves poverty like this, and yet, in a fallen world everyone is vulnerable to it. Jesus says, "The rain falls on the just and the unjust" (Matt. 5:45).

Yet, every day 30,000 children die of hunger and preventable diseases. Over 180 million people die unnecessarily each year from illnesses for which there are cures. There is no round-the-clock TV coverage for this silent, despairing travesty. Few will even notice. I pray those of us who still have breath will help make this kind of poverty history. Perhaps that is one of the reasons why we are still here. Together we can do it with the one who understands poverty like no other—one neighborhood at a time, if necessary.

Bono Again

Bono shouted to the crowd at Hyde Park, "We're not after charity. We're after justice!" Just over six months after the tsunami, the world made a statement that it wants to take poverty seriously. The Live 8 concerts led by Geldof and Bono went out to over 2 billion people. Not a fundraiser like the 1985 "Live Aid," the "Make Poverty History" campaign was about putting political pressure on the most powerful nations on earth. The so-called G8 listened to this global expression of the will of the people and promptly cancelled the debts of the world's poorest countries, doubled their aid budgets, and worked out a timetable for fairer trade.

I watched the G8 announcement by Tony Blair on TV only a few days after the Live 8 concert. It should have been one of the most exciting days of Blair's political career. He and thousands of others had worked hard for years for this result. Yet, a deep strain was etched on his face. He seemed close to tears, and there was no note of jubilation in his voice. Only a few days after the Live 8 concerts had packed up and the G8 summit was in full swing, one of the worst acts of terrorism in England's recent history occurred. Four bombs ripped through London's underground and a double-decker bus, leaving over fifty dead and hundreds injured.

Perhaps these events, together with May's and Saw's stories, show the reality of poverty. It can't be ended simply by powerful people pulling economic levers and switches—though this is needed as well. Even the power of mobilized billions and rock star celebrity power is not enough. Poverty and injustice is too sinister to be fooled by that. People had mobilized and shown their collective will, yet so too had a destructive force that could not be factored into the best laid plans to end poverty.

What will it take to end poverty? Jeffrey Sachs's book *The End of Poverty* has one of the most inspiring and optimistic forewords of any book I have read. Of course, it is by Bono. It says:

> We *can* be the generation that no longer accepts that an accident of latitude determines whether a child lives or dies—but *will* we be that generation? Will we in the West realize our potential or will we sleep in the comfort of our affluence with apathy and indifference murmuring softly in our ears?
>
> Sachs, *The End of Poverty*, xiv

Yet, there is something spiritual about poverty that can't be sorted out only by cash, economics, medicines, or government structures. Surely, despair is an integral part of poverty, and the only lasting antidote to despair is the hope that the living Christ can bring. My good friend Scott Bessenecker, who works with InterVarsity in helping American Christians engage with poverty, put it this way:

> Governments cannot grant true hope. We must acknowledge the spiritual dimension of poverty. There are also, I believe, demonic forces at work that the UN knows little about except in the most generic sense (greed, corruption, oppression are some of the faces but there are deep demonic roots). It will take discerning, spirit-filled people moving into these communities to confront demonic issues that surround poverty. Satan's plan in the garden was essentially a plan to perpetually impoverish God's image-bearers. One of God's original commands was to "subdue the earth." I think this relates to God's mission for humans to vanquish his enemy. Believers are called, equipped, and set apart to confront the powers of evil that keep people trapped in intractable poverty.

Jeffrey Sachs's book itself outlines a recipe that, if followed, claims to ensure the end of poverty—get people up to the next rung on the development ladder and they'll make the next one too, it argues. However, could it be that the book is far too materialistic and underestimates the stubborn spiritual reality and world view that oppresses those affected by poverty? Could it be that Christians could play a crucial role in ending the despair of poverty through the authority of the one who overcomes death?

From my experiences both in Melbourne and Bangkok, I know poverty and despair can become so internalized that it can take generations to heal. There is a family I know with four children who lives in Noble Park in Melbourne. No member of this family has had a meaningful job for two generations, and both parents and some grandparents have been in and out of jail. Getting a minimum wage job will not fix this. Just giving them enough to keep starvation at bay is not enough. Poverty is not just a lack of cash, medicine, or technology. It is also about the confidence, skills, and belief that people can use what they have for the community's good. Surely poverty is as much about identity, meaning, and belonging as material goods. Surely God's hope needs to be involved to change the world and rid it of poverty.

The Millennium Goals Are Not Enough

While I appreciate the sentiment, passion, and effort of the "Make Poverty History" campaign, in light of the above I wonder if the actual goals—known as the Millennium Development Goals—need to be revisited. These goals were put together by the United Nations and ratified by most countries. They aim to help quantify how and if poverty is being eradicated. But, as people of faith and hope, we should reconsider its definitions of poverty. For example, extreme poverty is defined as earning $1 a day, a nice figure dreamed up in a boardroom somewhere, but this has little to do with the complexities of real-life oppression or spirit-breaking despair. Such a definition can be helpful for those donating money, but it's hardly a measurement of whether poverty is being made history or not.

I question this measurement because:

24

It doesn't take urban realities seriously

For the first time in human history, most people now live in cities, including 1 billion people in slums (2 billion in slums by 2020, or one in four people). It is far more expensive to live in a city, and income can't be supplemented by growing or raising food; yet cities are where the majority of people are now going for jobs. In our slum (Klong Toey, Bangkok), $2 a day would rent you a tiny shack and nothing else. Living on $3 a day in our slum would be extreme poverty by any measure. Never mind what the poor actually need just to survive hunger in a Western city. There are simply too many variables in an increasingly urban world to measure poverty by per-day income.

It doesn't take poor families seriously

If a person living by him- or herself earns a dollar a day, it obviously would go further for him or her than it would for the sole breadwinner with a family of eleven. Because there is no social security safety net, and because infant mortality is high, the poor in the developing world often try to create as many children as possible. To fail to take this into account skews the count of those who live in poverty.

It doesn't take the nature of poverty seriously

While there have been far better attempts at measuring poverty with all its variables (e.g., the Henderson poverty line), even these become inadequate when the soft data of family background, disability, or age is included. As Christians we need to reread our Bibles and study such words as "oppression," for example. (There are, in fact, fourteen different Hebrew words for oppression.) What such a study reveals is that poverty by nature mars the image of God in people, and makes it impossible to live as God intends. The nature of poverty is as alive on the streets of Melbourne as it is in the slums of the developing world.

Of course, such definitions of poverty require responses to those oppressing and marring God's image, as well as measuring what minimum wage the oppressed need to keep hunger at bay. Making poverty history and stopping the oppression of the poor will require the giving up of wealth, power systems, and lifestyle privileges. Can we really make poverty history by taking these issues no more seriously than finding a neat measurement for the lowest possible income a poor person needs? Will we take poverty so personally that we really can make poverty history?

About This Series of Eight Bible Studies

Whereas my last two books, *Finding Life* and *Surrender All*, moved from our experiences in UNOH to scriptural reflections, this series of studies will follow a more traditionally evangelical route. Each of the eight chapters in this book reflects on responses to poverty in key biblical texts, with consideration given to their literary contexts. Each chapter begins with an opening reflection to help the reader enter the world of the Bible, and then we engage with some of the specific biblical concerns related to poverty. Only then does this lead to some reflection on personal and community experiences I have had, both here in Klong Toey and in Melbourne. Finally, I provide some suggestions for practical action, as well as questions for group discussion.

This book is aimed particularly at those who have a sneaking suspicion that the Christian faith is more than a cultural ornament, that it is a call to follow Jesus as he stands in solidarity with the poor. I have been asked numerous times to recommend a book accessible to ordinary Christians that would help small groups engage in a Bible study about poverty. My prayer is that this book can be an answer to such a request.

I pray that you will see the biblical writing on the wall and make a response. "Saw" in my opening story might be a figment of my imagination, but the awful truth he represents, and his plea for us to stand with him, is a truth that both billions living in poverty and the God of the Bible want us to see, hear, and act upon.

I pray also that this book contributes to the undermining of the Western use of the Bible as an ornament for admiration, or even as a mat to stand on. May its intricately woven threads combine again to cause the revolutionary action for which it truly calls. If one more Saw of this world is heard and stood with, then this book will have done its job.

How to Get the Most Out of This Book

This book will change and inspire if you:

- have a small group of people willing to journey together no matter where Jesus leads;
- pray for an openness to the Spirit who inspired all Scripture and inspires us today to see insights and act upon them;
- get to know actual people who are facing poverty and stand with them against their exploitation and injustices;
- agree to read a chapter of the book and the Bible passages before you come together as a group so that you can all work off the same page. You can then, with better insight as a community, reflect on the "group questions."

With two-thirds of the world living in poverty, the Bible's message has never been more important. I pray we can each see, hear, and find our responses to the Bible's call for us to stand with the poor.

Lord, please help us to take poverty as personally as you do!

1

Beyond Excuses

Moses, the Exodus, and Courage to Face the Nature of Poverty

Opening Reflection: God, Please Do Something!

Henry clung to his orange life jacket, bobbing up and down in the icy-cold water, surveyed the thousands of pieces of fiberglass and plastic floating around him that used to be his prized speedboat, and prayed, "Lord, please save me. I believe you will save me."

Deep in his heart Henry sensed God answer, "I will save you, my son."

A few minutes later a banana boat appeared at the horizon. It sped towards him. The driver yelled out, "Do you want some help?"

"No thanks," Henry replied, "my God said he would save me." The banana boat sped back to shore.

A few hours later Henry drifted out into the deep ocean currents. He still clung to his orange life jacket and now his teeth started to chatter together with the cold. Just then, a Russian oil tanker sailed by. One of the crew spotted Henry and threw over a rope. "Grab the rope and we'll save you," the captain said over the PA.

"No, my God said he would save me." Not being able to stop, the tanker had no choice but to cruise by.

Another two hours went by, and by this time Henry had started to turn a pasty blue color. A helicopter appeared on the horizon, flew towards Henry, and a rope was let down.

From a loudspeaker the chopper pilot called out, "Grab the rope and we'll save you."

Still Henry clung onto his orange life jacket and waved his hands to refuse help. "No, my God said he would save me." The helicopter had limited fuel in the middle of nowhere; it could not stay for long, and had to fly off.

A few hours later Henry blacked out and died, still clinging onto his orange life jacket.

In an instant Henry was ushered into the throne room of God. His cheeks returning to a bright red color, Henry stormed up to God and demanded, "I trusted you. I believed you when you said you would save me. Why didn't you save me?"

"Hey," said the Lord, "I sent you a banana boat, an oil tanker, and a helicopter. What more did you want from me?"

✝

Henry's story is one of my favorite humorous stories. Maybe it's not what you were expecting to open a chapter in a book about poverty, but, like all good humor, it has some truth. In this case, it is that some people think God should fix problems—such as poverty and the state of the world—in his own cosmic way, without people. But as we shall see from the life of Moses, we all have our part to play. We all need to do something.

Courage is a word that literally means "from the heart." Traditionally, courage was believed to be the only virtue that could

29

overcome doubt and fear. If God is to save the world, the part each of us is required to play in both giving and taking help as God's answers to prayer will require courage.

My prayer is that these reflections on Moses will give us courage to trust an extraordinary God, who is above the pressures the world places on us, and be his answers in the world. I pray that we will make poverty personal and not simply look to others to do it for us.

The Bible's Call: Moses's Impact

We cannot understand the Bible unless we have a deep appreciation of Moses and the exodus event. The first five books of the Old Testament are called the "Books of Moses" because traditionally they are attributed to Moses and his point of view.

The first book, Genesis, describes the origins of Moses's people, the Hebrews. It includes an account of how God created the world, the creation of humanity in God's image, the fall of this state, and then, as a response to the fall, the founding of the Hebrew nation through Abraham. After the outline of the origins of the Hebrews, the book of Exodus shows the defining event of the nation—how God liberated the Hebrew people from slavery.

The rest of the Old Testament includes laws, history, poetry, and the writings of the prophets, which are essentially a call to be faithful to the One who freed the Hebrew people from slavery in the exodus and brought them to the Promised Land. To miss the significance of the exodus event, then, is to miss a foundational building block of our faith.

What do you think of when Moses and the exodus are mentioned? A Sunday school moment when you cut Moses out of cardboard? The old movie image of Charlton Heston's flowing white beard and his staff held defiantly above his head (a better image than the rifle he often held above his head at gun rallies in later life!) as the Red Sea parted to dramatic orchestral music?

30

Perhaps, if you are younger, you think of the cartoon version of *The Prince of Egypt*, with its gruesome plagues and Whitney Houston songs (I'm not sure which is more gruesome!). While the story has captivated many generations in different ways, to find the courage to be faithful to the Lord in these times we should not let the exodus story become a child's play, a Hollywood classic, or a cartoon. We need to re-engage with this ancient, foundational story, and allow the Exodus event, and Moses's life in particular, to impact our lives today.

Imagination Exercise: Become a Slave

Read this story, imagining you are a slave:

There are specks of sand stinging your eyes. Your muscles are tender and fatigued. You're afraid to look up into your master's eyes in case you are whipped again. Your life, that of your family, and those of at least one million of your people are, for the most part, out of your hands. Your battle each day, as you follow orders moving huge rocks and sand, is just survival—just to get through each day, every day, for years.

You arrive home to your shack and see your kids asleep already. This is not only your lot, but also will be theirs and their children's as well.

This was the life of the majority of the Hebrews when the exodus event took place. Imagine crying out to God in this predicament. What would you scream?

You have heard about Moses. He was not a slave like you, though. Sure, he was born a Hebrew, but when a massacre of Hebrew children occurred, he was pushed out onto the river by his mother and taken in by an Egyptian princess. Moses had grown up in a palace, and had been fostered and raised by the princess and her entourage. You have heard also that Moses had killed an Egyptian in frustration at the treatment of his own Hebrew people, and that he is now a tragic fugitive who is wandering through the desert.

What if your prayers are being answered through this man Moses? What if God is talking with Moses about your freedom right now?

As a slave, read Exodus 3:1–4:17, eavesdropping on this conversation between the Lord and Moses. How do you feel, hearing this conversation? Relief—that God has heard your cry? Anger—at Moses, for, even though God has spoken to him through a tree on fire, he doesn't want to get involved? Fear—that God is relying on such a reluctant figure to do something about your situation?

While there is a real hope offered for change and a better future here, there is also a vulnerability and humanness about it. The hope may not be realized if Moses doesn't get with the program. Certainly Moses doesn't look like the answer to your prayers.

Though understandable from the perspective of God and the slave, anger cannot be our final feeling about the reluctant Moses. We would only feel anger at ourselves. Unless we can tap into the hope for something more, in Moses (and in ourselves), we may just wallow in our own guilt, despair, and shame—and nothing will actually change.

The God of Moses doesn't just want us to be down on ourselves, but for us to look beyond ourselves and trust in him. Freedom from suffering only comes when God inspires ordinary people to do extraordinary things. This is where change happens. Are we ready to move beyond excuses?

Moses, Excuses, and God's Response to Poverty

To follow the theme of God's response to poverty, consider each of Moses's five excuses to God for not getting involved. Could they also be our own excuses for not making deeper responses to those facing oppression and injustice? Could they be our excuses for not being answers to our own prayers and the prayers of the poor?

Excuse one: Who do you think I am? (Exodus 3:1–12)

The Lord knew Moses by name. "Moses, Moses," he called out through a flaming wilderness shrub. Shaken, Moses could only respond, "Here I am." People might think they would love a personal experience of the God who really knows them inside out, but often this is a vague, romantic feeling about God, neither biblically authentic nor true to human experience. Moses certainly did not feel warm fuzzies about God in front of the burning bush. This was not the sentimentalized experience of God contained in so many contemporary Christian worship songs that have "Here I am, Lord" in them. Moses was summoned by the almighty, creator God, and he could only squeak out the obvious.

What God related to Moses was a directive more dangerous, and yet more adventurous, than anything Moses could have imagined. God really had "heard the cries" of his Hebrew people who were "in misery" and wanted Moses to free his people from this oppression.

At this point it is interesting to note this word "oppression" as it occurs in the Hebrew Bible. There are no less than nine main words for oppression weaved throughout the Old Testament. Because of the slavery of the Hebrews, and God's concern for them, these words need deep reflection if we are to understand poverty:

- *anah*—In Genesis 15:13 God said to Abram, "Know this for certain, that your offspring shall be aliens in a land that is not theirs, and shall be slaves there, and they shall be oppressed (*anah*) for four hundred years." (See also Exod. 1:11; 2 Sam. 13:12; Ps. 119:75; Isa. 53:4.) This word *anah* has to do with the tyranny of the powerful, the degradation of people, and even the violent sexual exploitation of women.
- *ashaq*—Micah 2:1–2 says, "Alas for those who devise wickedness and evil deeds on their beds! When the morning dawns, they perform it, because it is in their power. They covet fields, and seize them; houses, and take them away; they oppress (*ashaq*) householder and house, people and

their inheritance." (See also Lev. 19:13; Hos. 12:7.) Because the people have no authority, their fields, savings, capital, and even homes are taken in violent and unjust ways without recourse.

- *lachats*—In Exodus 3:9–10 God tells Moses, "The cry of the Israelites has now come to me; I have also seen how the Egyptians oppress (*lachats*) them. So come, I will send you to Pharaoh to bring my people, the Israelites, out of Egypt." (See also 1 Kings 22:27; Jer. 30:19–21; Isa. 19:20; Amos 6:14.) The Egyptians are crushing the Hebrews; God hears their cries and wants to respond by freeing them. This is about a lack of freedom from grinding injustice.

- *nagas*—In Isaiah 3:5–6 the prophet says, "The people will be oppressed (*nagas*), everyone by another and everyone by a neighbor; the youth will be insolent to the elder, and the base to the honorable." (See also Exod. 5:6–14; 2 Kings 23:35; Job 39:7.) This word is about forced labor, oppression, and exploitation.

- *yanah*—In Ezekiel 45:8 we read, "And my princes shall no longer oppress (*yanah*) my people." (See also Lev. 25:14; Ezek. 46:18; Zeph. 3:1.) Again this word is about oppression and violence against those who are not in a position to defend themselves.

- *ratsats*—Job 20:19 says, "For they have crushed (*ratsats*) and abandoned the poor, they have seized a house that they did not build." (See also Isa. 58:6; Jer. 22:17.) This is crushing, isolating, and despoiling the poor, including stripping them bare and taking their homes.

- *dakka*—Psalm 94:5–7 says, "They crush (*dakka*) your people, O Lord, and afflict your heritage. They kill the widow and the stranger, they murder the orphan, and they say, 'The Lord does not see; the God of Jacob does not perceive.'" In arrogance the powerful "crush" God's people, oppressing them, killing the most vulnerable and falsely believing that God does not see. But God does see and will act.

34

- *dak*—Psalm 74:21 says, "Do not let the downtrodden (*dak*) be put to shame; let the poor and needy praise your name." (See also Ps. 10:18.) This word is about treading upon the heads of the poor and oppressing and putting down the needy.
- *tok*—Psalm 10:7 says, "Their mouths are filled with cursing and deceit and oppression (*tok*); under their tongues are mischief and iniquity." (See also Ps. 55:11; 72:14.) This word *tok* is about the powerful causing violent injury to those who are helpless.

What are the common themes here that can help us understand the nature of poverty? Certainly, poverty includes destitution and requires finding ways to respond to those who are crushed and down and out; yet, a Hebrew understanding of poverty is much broader than simply destitution. It has to do with oppression and the life God intends for those being crushed, who are made in God's image. A Hebrew understanding of poverty, then, is not just about destitution. It is by nature a lack of ability to live as God intends. How does God intend those made in his image to live? God's liberation from oppression for the Hebrew people included the promise that they would live in "a land flowing with milk and honey," symbols of a sustainable and joyful life. Poverty, then, is about a lack of freedom to choose God's *shalom*, to live a meaningful life. This kind of poverty faces the majority of the planet today and provides a starting point in understanding how we can respond to poverty. It is this definition of poverty that informed Jesus's understanding of his mission "to bring good news to the poor" (Luke 4:18–19).

The Lord says to Moses, "So come, I will send you to Pharaoh to bring my people, the Israelites, out of Egypt." Moses, however, knew his people and the dictator Pharaoh. Cowering in the sand, Moses said to God, "Who am I that I should go to Pharaoh, and bring the Israelites out of Egypt?"

If you were a slave watching this conversation, couldn't you have put your hands around Moses's neck at this point? I mean, who are you, Moses? You're the one who grew up in a palace. You know Pharaoh and his people personally. You are the only one of us who has lived out in this desert and knows how to survive and travel beyond slavery to the new land. Moses, everything in your life has been shaped for this. Now you have this awe-inspiring summons from the Almighty! Throw your lot in with us and you will be part of history! If you are not prepared to do this, then who can God use?

God was impatient, too. He expressed clearly his passion for his suffering people. "I will be with you; and this shall be the sign for you that it is I who sent you: when you have brought the people out of Egypt, you shall worship God on this mountain." God's presence in people is what makes a difference. When it was all over, God promised his free people would come back to this very mountain to worship the Lord freely, without fear of others. Moses, too, would come back here a free person, no longer a fugitive. This is real hope in the face of despair— that despite everything, God will keep his promise and free his people.

It can be too easy to look at ourselves and make excuses—not good enough, not spiritual enough, not young enough, not old enough, not smart enough, not enough time or energy. Yet, as we see in Moses, the life of faith is not about our own deservedness, but about the goodness of the Lord. The Lord hears the cries of the oppressed, his heart breaks, and he picks people out— flawed people like you and me and Moses—to be his response. Indeed, flawed people are the only kind of people God has to work with.

Margaret Mead once said, "Never doubt that a small group of thoughtful, committed citizens can change the world. Indeed, it is the only thing that ever has." Moses was not thoughtful, committed, or prepared to work with others at this point; but God could change all that, and thus change the world. Throughout history this has proved to be something of the Lord's specialty!

God knows each of us, and the way we are shaped as people is no accident. One of the main reasons we have the book of Genesis

36

is not to satisfy our curiosity as to how God made the world, but to give the origins of how God liberated real people from slavery. Those who were made in God's image, but fallen, became a nation. Latin American theologian Georges Casalis puts it this way:

> The heart of the Old Testament is the Exodus from the servitude of Egypt and the journey to the promised land. . . . The hope of the people of God is not to regain paradise lost, but to march forward towards a new city, a human and brotherly [and sisterly] city whose heart is Christ.
>
> Cited in Gustavo Gutiérrez, A *Theology of Liberation,* 157

As Moses's life shows, God wastes no experience in moving us toward this freedom. Everything and anything can be helpful to enable true liberation to be possible for us, and through us to others. Our pain, mistakes, and even our "palace" experiences or powerless times can be transformed by God to help others. God needs all kinds of people to make our communities and world a better place.

God has his hand on each of our lives. If we stay close to God, and respond to God's summons and promises, we may, like Moses, return to some of the old places—commissioning mountains, even—where we have been before, but we come back as liberated people. We can fulfill our reason for being born. Being animated by the presence of the Lord is enough to make amazing contributions to this life, far beyond our own reckonings. The real question is, Will we trust God with who he has made us to be?

Excuse two: Who are you really, Lord? (Exodus 3:13–22)

The second excuse is about theology. When Moses asked for God's name, he was not simply thinking they hadn't been properly introduced yet. When Hebrew people asked someone for their name, they were really asking what kind of person they were. For example, "What is your name?" Jacob is asked in Genesis 32:27. When he answers "Jacob," the response is,

37

"You shall no longer be called Jacob, but Israel." This change from Jacob (literally meaning "to seize by the heel," as he did in the womb with his brother Esau, or figuratively, "one who overreaches in life") to Israel (meaning "one who wrestles with God") illustrates what can happen when God changes the very nature of a person. God changes the names of all kinds of people throughout the Bible to catch up with God's transforming work in their lives.

What, then, does the story of the burning bush tell us about what God is like? Moses had taken off his sandals, signifying that he felt it was a sacred place. He had cowered in the sand as he talked with a bush on fire, overwhelmed by the presence of God. The Lord knew Moses by name and summoned him on a mission. Moses surely had experienced what God was like, so I doubt this second excuse was about knowing God or even an effort to get into a clever debate about theology with God. What God is like goes beyond mere words. What is true about this excuse is that we mere creatures often need metaphors to help us and others make sense of our creator.

The creator God could not fully answer Moses's question. A creator, by definition, is other than what the creation is or can even imagine. The Lord is, however, able to communicate with his creation in ways that give a glimpse into his nature. The Lord explained to Moses what he was like by looking back and pointing out where he had intervened and shaped people and events in his nation's history (Exod. 3:15). The Lord then pointed to the present, where his heart was breaking over the misery of his people (Exod. 3:16–17).

He then predicted the future of a new land that would provide everything they would need to live well (Exod. 3:18–22). The summary name of God, then, is "I AM WHO I AM" (Exod. 3:14). A being beyond time and space, yet one who intervenes personally in human history in an ever-present way. There is no way we humans can tame this being, even if we try to do so with our imaginations.

The Lord revealed himself in a way that challenged Moses and the Hebrew people's understanding of God. He asked Moses to remember his story, and this reveals a glimpse of the nature of God: a deeply compassionate God who chose people like Abraham, Isaac, and Jacob to be his instruments of mercy for a better future; a God with emotion and pathos, who felt deeply in his bones and then responded; a God who took sides against oppression and the perpetrators of that oppression; a God who shaped the world through being present in the people who were open and available to him.

But if God is so powerful, why doesn't he do something about all the evil and suffering in the world? How many times do Christians hear this very real question? The story of Moses's encounter with God at the burning bush answers this question in part by suggesting that while people are the ones responsible for the mess we are in, God also looks for people that he can use to clean it up. Humans—the creatures made in God's image—are God's answer to the problems in the world. The invisible hand of God is placed on people and he longs for people to respond and be available to his direction. Will we trust this God to use us as his answers to a suffering world?

Excuse three: What will people think? (Exodus 4:1–9)

Moses's third excuse was about credibility with the people he actually feared most—other Hebrews. He was more concerned about his peers and kin than his Egyptian adversaries, or even the Lord himself. "But suppose they do not believe me or listen to me, but say, 'The Lord did not appear to you.'" Reputations, egos, and projected images of who we think we ought to be can undermine our confidence in the Lord. God spoke through a burning bush and spelled out clearly to Moses what needed to be done, but "What will people think?" was an internalized, default position that Moses was honest enough to verbalize.

Sometimes the opinions and voices we value most can override even our most authentic faith experiences. What will mom and dad think of this? What will my friends say? Will my teachers approve? Even an experience like facing God and hearing his audible voice in a burning bush can become unbelievable to us if those whose opinions matter most drown that experience out. It is acceptable for most people to try "a little bit of religion" to help them get what they want and need. For many, it is rarely acceptable to surrender all they are to God, including their reputations, and risk being branded a traitor, an expatriate, or a religious terrorist. Or even worse, for some—will our neighbors think that the "born again nerd" (i.e., Ned Flanders from *The Simpsons*) has moved in? Yet, Moses and those who have changed the world have had to live with these kinds of labels, and worse. It takes some ego-strength to trust God above all the other voices telling us what we ought to be like.

Some of my Thai neighbors have a hard time with family and friends for being a Christian. Losing your support network is a huge thing anywhere, but in Thailand it also can be a welfare issue. Culturally, a mother rejecting a son is one of the most tragic circumstances in Thailand. Sometimes the rejection is not because of what God is actually like, but rather perceptions. For example, in Thailand it generally is considered that Jesus was a *farung* (Westerner) and that following Jesus is therefore only for *farungs*. (This, despite the fact that there are more Christians in developing countries than in the West today.) Thai Christians don't help—one of the most often-used paintings of Jesus in churches here is one of a Jesus with long, light-brown hair and bright-blue eyes. I call this painting "Jesus the Californian"—it illustrates the foreignness of Jesus, who actually has more in common with the average Thai than they realize.

I once preached from this passage about Moses in the Ta Rua church in the Klong Toey slum. I remember looking up at the thirty or so tired and faithful souls when I got to this section. "I know some of you have been cut off from family because they think Christianity is only for *farungs*. Some don't think well of you because you've joined a *farung* religion. But Jesus was not a *farung*. As a descendant from Hebrew slaves, he would have had much darker skin than I have. In the time of Jesus, the Hebrews were overwhelmed by Roman powers and had to fight to keep their culture and customs from being swamped by a foreign one. Jesus grew up in a place called Galilee, which was far more like Klong Toey than any Western city. In these ways and more, Jesus was far more like a Thai than a *farung*. Following Jesus can enable Thais to be free to be the unique people God intends Thais to be. Still, it takes courage to follow that path, and I can't pretend to know the costs you make and keep making to stand with Jesus."

I believe Thais have a unique role to play in the world and for our faith. It is one of the reasons we have helped to set up a sister-church relationship between Ta Rua and some Australian churches. Jesus wants Aussies to live as God intends, too, and over the next few years, hopefully we can share our unique cultures, customs, and gifts, which will in turn shape our common faith and life together. I concluded the sermon, "You have a crucial role to play in the world. Only you can be true to God in this community. Others will find their freedom, too, because you have something special and unique to offer the world." The congregation clapped at that point.

God knew what people would think of Moses, and yet would not let him off his responsibilities that easily. What people think—true or false—of our faith experience shouldn't matter to us. Doing what's right is what matters. Doing what God wants should matter most. Ultimately, it is to God we have to give account of what we have done with our lives.

God honored Moses. He turned everyday items into help so that Moses could have confidence with others in this adventure of faith. His shepherd's crook could be turned into a venomous snake, and then back into a crook. If Moses put his hand inside his coat, it would turn leprous. If he put his hand inside a second time, the leprosy was gone. The Lord promised that if Moses got a bucket of the Nile's water, it would be turned into blood as soon as it hit the dry ground. These were breath-taking signs and wonders by any measurement.

Yet, even these tricks didn't convince Moses, and he knew it wouldn't calm the people he feared. Moses would quickly move on to the next excuse.

God can transform miraculously our everyday work tools (like crooks), bodies (like hands), and even life sources (like blood) to be scary warning signs to others that God is serious about this world. Yet, mostly, God chooses not to. If God did this for us at will, we would probably feel even weirder and less able to convince others! Change actually comes from solidarity with and being alongside of God—not what tricks we can do from on high. We see this clearly in the God who becomes flesh and blood and moves into the neighborhood.

It is true that God may give us some tricks to do at times, but that will not give us the inner conviction to look beyond the opinions and labels others may have of us. Confidence comes from a simple trust and obedience in the one who says, "I am who I am." It is his opinion of us that counts both now and when the world ends, when everyone knows everything.

What is of eternal value is rarely cool or popular or acceptable; it has not been otherwise at any given time in human history. I doubt that on that final day of history many will want to be like Brad Pitt or Britney Spears or Thailand's pop star Tata Young—who may even have lost their popularity and funkiness! Will we have the courage to recognize God and respond, even if others think less of us at this time?

Excuse four: What skills do I really have for this? (Exodus 4:10–12)

Moses said, "O my Lord, I have never been eloquent, neither in the past nor even now that you have spoken to your servant; but I am slow of speech and slow of tongue." He pointed out the obvious here—clearly, Moses was not skilled or special enough for a quest like this. No one could have enough skills to topple the most powerful empire in the then-known world.

The obvious, however, does not allow for God's grace.

The Lord responded directly to Moses's fourth excuse. "Who gives speech to mortals? Who makes them mute or deaf, seeing or blind? Is it not I, the LORD? Now go, and I will be with your mouth and teach you what you are to speak." Particular skills such as speaking or the lack of them are not the issue here—the Lord is. For the Lord is the originator, able to go ahead and prepare hearts and lives for us. The creator God is behind all communication, opening (and closing) all ears, mouths, and hearts to truth.

No human being is any more exceptional than another. This is especially the case when God wants to use humans to be an answer to the misery and suffering over which he weeps. This is not to say that we don't have to work hard at identifying and nurturing the skills our unique callings require, but what is required to end poverty ultimately comes from God. It is God who is exceptional, not us. Like Moses, we need to depend on the giver of the gifts, not just get caught up wondering what gifts are required.

As we go on in life, God gives us the grace and gifts to do what is required. One of my favorite Corrie Ten Boom stories is of people questioning her about hiding Jewish people in her home from the Nazis or how she coped in a concentration camp. They would say, "I could never do that." Corrie would just smile, "You can't buy the grace ticket in advance. It's only once on board the train that you can get the grace ticket. You don't need it until then."

I wonder how many people do not get involved with the suffering of others because they want the grace ticket in advance. "I can't speak well enough," or "I can't do anything about that," or "I don't have enough of a heart for those people" become the basic assumptions rather than the grace of God.

Like Moses, we can scare ourselves by trying to imagine ourselves in future places for which God has not yet given us grace. So we miss out on the ride of our lives and end up only living cautiously.

Excuse five: Surely someone else can do this? (Exodus 4:13–17)

Moses exhausted his list of excuses to the one speaking from a bush on fire. The only thing left was to mutter out loud what many Christians in the world today whisper in their hearts: "O my Lord, please send someone else." Despite signs, wonders, and promises given by the Lord, Moses wanted someone else to get involved. Moses wanted to raise his young family, keep working, and live as normal a life as possible. While this excuse was a rational one—of course there were other people God could have raised up—it was this excuse that got the strongest reaction from the Lord. It might just have been the culminating effect that this fifth excuse brought, but as you imagined this story unfolding from the perspective of the slave in the opening reflection, perhaps it was this statement that you most reacted to as well.

The text actually says, "The anger of the LORD was kindled against Moses." This was to have long-term, tangible consequences for Moses. The Lord was not some kind of super machine to be switched on and off. Rather, the Lord revealed a deep passion, expressing deep feelings about the detachment of his people and Moses. The Lord was deeply hurt, and his frustration boiled over. Do anything, this text seems to say, but don't take God's patience for granted.

Still angry, the Lord worked out a solution with Moses. "What of your brother Aaron, the Levite? I know that he can speak fluently . . . he shall serve as a mouth for you, and you shall serve as God for him. Take in your hand this staff, with which you shall perform the signs." The Lord arranged for Aaron to partner with Moses. While such a partnership would have its problems, it is a good example of the way God can bring people together, contributing strengths to others' weaknesses. Aaron could speak well, and Moses felt he needed this.

There is a sense in which we all need an Aaron. As the journey unfolds, we need to rely on other people with gifts we don't feel we have. So, yes, the Lord can sometimes negotiate with us in all this, but we can't take it for granted that it will have no effect on our lives. "Anger" was "kindled" by the Lord towards Moses: a fire was being prepared that was far more terrifying than the one that didn't burn the negotiating bush. This was a real relationship with a God of passion and frustration, not simply a ghostlike transaction to get things done.

44

Should we look for others? Yes, we should, and there probably are people—like an Aaron—we know already who can go on this journey with us. There are people we can contact. There are people who can bring to the table things we cannot. The role of sister churches helps here, providing cash and support. However, Moses's interaction with God teaches us that we can't avoid playing our own part. We can't wait for others to do it all for us, lest the anger of the Lord is kindled against us, too.

✝

Moses came up with five excuses in quick succession. Which of these do you most relate to when it comes to responding to poverty? Most of us only require one or two to legitimize watching from the sidelines, or clinging to our orange life jacket. We live in an age where justifying almost anything to ourselves is an art form and few know of our burning-bush excuses. However, such excuses don't wash with the Lord.

The Exodus story reveals a passionate God who responds to and is not neutral on situations of suffering and injustice. We may not all get a burning-bush summons today, but we do have the Bible, whose revelation is miraculous. With God's grace, can we respond faithfully and with integrity, transforming situations of suffering? What is required is simply "a commitment to act." Will we be open to do whatever it takes?

As reluctant as Moses was, he was used by the Lord to change the course of human history. He initially felt he wasn't really able to do this, but God gave him the grace to make a unique and powerful contribution, far beyond any natural skills he had to offer. God did open the ears, eyes, and hearts of both those suffering and those causing suffering. Eventually, the Hebrews worked long enough together to become an alternative, liberated community that pointed the whole world to God.

Imagine if Moses had believed his own excuses. The world would be a different place. It is the same for us. Don't believe the self-preserving and self-justifying voices in our heads. They are most probably wrong. Moses never did get to the Promised Land, but he did make a unique and lasting contribution, inspiring us to this day. We may never see our community living the kind of life we want, but perhaps we can play our part. Can we, like Moses, move beyond our excuses to live out our faith, participating in changing the suffering of those around us? What on heaven or earth can stop us?

Personal Reflection: The Courage to Contribute

In an image-conscious world, it takes courage to make our contributions. Witness the new neighborhood house and worship center that opened deep in the heart of Penung slum in 2003. The aroma of green curry boiling away in the corner was just overcoming that of the seventy sweating bodies crammed into the center's lower-level room. The blue ribbon was cut, and it fell between two rough brick pillars with dry concrete oozing out, hand built by the pastor himself, watched by a mixture of residents and church people in T-shirts, Korean sponsors in ceremonial church dresses, and me in my best (but sweat-soaked) Colorado shirt and flip flops. Immediately the crowd erupted, the room seeming to bow outwards, with hoots and clapping. No sooner had the ribbon been cut and the room returned to its intended shape than we were all ushered up the metal ladderlike stairs, cramming into the upstairs worship room, the walls still sticky and pungent from fresh paint.

My highlight of the night was soon to appear—the dancing girls! As the crackling tape forced out some traditional Thai stringed music, seven shimmering beauties in gold and silver traditional dresses and featherlike headpieces swayed their bodies and twisted their fingers backwards into impossible positions. These were no ordinary, heavily made up dancing girls, however—none of them was under seventy years old! As soon as they appeared, those in the crowded worship room smiled together at once, and a sense of serenity and belonging descended. By the end of the night just about everyone in the room had participated in some way. Even a

group from 70 Rye (another part of Klong Toey slum) had organized themselves into a choir. What was remarkable about this
was that many had disabilities of an oral nature and sang with
saliva dribbling from one side of their mouths.

It was hard not to compare these contributions with what I had
noticed on a recent trip to Australia. After speaking in a number
of different churches (Baptist, Churches of Christ, Anglican, and
Pentecostal) I was struck by the similarities in the worship events.
It wasn't just that they sang the same songs. (What does God
giving us "the nations" and "distant shores and islands" mean,
anyway? New holiday destinations or real estate opportunities?)
It was that it seemed only skinny, well-groomed people out of
Vogue magazine were allowed to sing up front. Of course, then I
would waddle up, try to spit out what I had to say, and spoil the
picture-perfect image.

I know there is an argument about the need for relevance and
accessibility for the television generation, but in the Penung slum
experience the focus was on participation. Performance was secondary. It wasn't contrived at all—few wished they could look and
act like these old ladies or singers with disabilities.

It was, however, inspirational. If a group like that could dance
or sing in front of people, we could all contribute something!
I wonder if that possibility is just as accessible, relevant, and
perhaps more faithful to kingdom values as any.

Please do not misunderstand me. I am not arguing here to
stop skinny people from singing up front in church—they at
least are participating. Nor is this a call for a kind of affirma-
tive action plan for all the non–Elle McPhersons of the church
to sing. Congregations would soon play "spot the token ugly
duckling." But if those with talent to help congregations sing are
not encouraged or given opportunity because of image, I think
that is a sin. What I really wonder is if a form and style copied
from television and the theater could be stopping many people
from feeling like they can make a contribution. "Lord, I don't
really have the skills, image, and confidence for this." Does the
tiny proportion of people involved in ministry compared to the

number who watch it all happen safely from a distance have something to do with the images that are being projected (and thus valued) consciously and subconsciously by our churches? Could this amplify the excuses for lack of involvement and make it easier to opt out?

In such a climate, the excuses Moses used not to get involved are often the default excuses we can use today. Who, me? Who are you really, Lord? What will people think? What skills do I really have? Can't someone else do it? These voices are internalized and conspire to undermine our capacity to make our unique contribution to the miseries of the world. Our contribution may not be holding staffs in front of seas and armies, liberating a nation, but it takes just as much courage to do what God has called each of us to do, given the pressures not to do it.

Questions arise for us from all this, not least of which is, How are we going to contribute and model good news for the poor this year? This is a central aspect of following Jesus (Luke 4:18–19). I doubt we need to hold up more supermodel-like people to aspire to—society already does that, creating insecurities in many of us.

We do, however, need to become more inspiring people ourselves, willing to take risks with our fragile egos, offering everything we have to Jesus and the poor so close to God's heart.

Today many of the world's poorest—those oppressed with little or no authority to choose to live as God intends—know the Christian's claim that God instructs them to "love their neighbors as themselves." Indeed, a book more miraculously put together than any tree on fire is claimed to command this. Yet the poor are waiting to see the evidence that this can be true. Can we, like Moses, move beyond our excuses to live out our faith, participating in changing the hurting world around us? What on heaven or earth can stop us?

Bring on more dancing girls (and saliva singers)!

Questions for Discussion

Critical questions

- What does this story reveal about what Moses was like?
- What does this story reveal about what God is like?
- What is the nature of poverty in this story?
- How did God respond to the excuses Moses gave for not getting involved in helping to liberate his people?

Amplifying questions

- If you were Moses, how would you have felt about this encounter with the Lord?
- Which of Moses's excuses for not contributing can you relate to most, and why?

A Personal Exercise

Write what a "slave" of our day would see and hear of our lives. Have an imaginary conversation with this slave through writing. Listen, too, to what the slave says back to you, for it may be the voice of God disguised!

2

Hebrew Laws and "Always Having" Poverty

Opening Reflection: The Jubilee Laws

Again God spoke to Moses on Mount Sinai. Miraculously, the Hebrews had escaped Egypt through various plagues on their oppressors and through the Red Sea. Then, as God had promised, Moses returned to the peak of the same mountain where, when he was a fugitive, he had been called through a burning bush to free his people from misery. On Mount Sinai, the Lord outlined the basic expectations and a code to live by, not just for Moses but also for his emerging, liberated nation.

A good example of this code is the jubilee laws. Take some time to reflect on these laws, perhaps still the most radical laws to combat poverty ever conceived. Written over 3,000 years ago when the strongest of the world were killing and maiming at will, these laws were remarkable because everyone from the most powerful to the least powerful were to be subject to them. They still have something to say to us today.

Take a few minutes to be silently attentive to the presence of the living God and, once still, to read quietly these verses three times in full. Let the Lord hit you with any phrase he wills, and dwell on its meaning with him.

Read Leviticus 25:8–55. What most strikes you about these laws?

To read these laws is to see what is possible for today's world. People such as Bono and others from the Jubilee 2000 group were so inspired by these verses that they took up a campaign to combat Third World debt.

It was one thing for the Hebrews to defeat an enemy and topple oppression; it was quite another to develop a community able to be God's people in the world, staying true to the liberation they had experienced. God, therefore, provided a whole range of laws and commandments, setting out a code to live by so that the oppressed did not quickly become oppressors.

The Bible's Call: The Two Main Concerns of Mosaic Law

We will come back to consider the jubilee laws more fully later in this chapter, but at this point we need to look at the core of the Mosaic laws—the Ten Commandments.

Like most of the Hebrew legal code, the Ten Commandments had two special concerns. The first concern was to ensure that the Hebrews stayed close to the living God—to love God with their whole being. The creation of images that represented "gods" that humans felt they needed was not permitted. To create or try to domesticate a god to justify wrongdoing or to try to manipulate it to get what they wanted was not permitted. As we will see in chapter 4, the prophets would later take up these issues of faithfulness to God and not making idols with wild eyes and lives.

The second concern of these laws was to restrain the powerful and protect those who were weakest among them, so that all could live in health and peace—that is, to love their neighbors. At the heart of this second command is a public recognition of the selfishness of the human heart. We do—or don't do—things to, with, and for others because we get an advantage from them, and this is against God's intentions for us. Therefore, working people seven days a week like slaves is not God's intention; hence the requirement of a Sabbath day to ensure this doesn't happen. To be jealous of neighbors is to be discontent with what you already have, and this is not caring deeply for your neighbor or yourself. To kill a neighbor is not to love them, either. How we treat "the other," then, not only reflects how we really relate to God, but also underscores how we understand ourselves and our own power. This goes back to the creation story, which indicates that people are not gods—as many powerful people of that age acted—yet neither are they subhuman and to be treated like animals. All those made in God's image need to be treated with respect and dignity.

The laws outlined in Leviticus 19 and their equivalents in Deuteronomy have a whole range of community laws that are about protecting the weakest in society and restraining the most powerful. Imagine if the spirit of these laws was evoked today. What would the world look like if each community was proactive in remembering the poor in daily life (Lev. 19:9–10; Deut. 24:19–22), wages for workers were paid fairly (Lev. 19:13; Deut. 24:14–15), justice for each person was upheld (Lev. 19:15; Deut. 16:18-20), care and responsibility was taken in the interest of others (Lev. 19:16–18; Deut. 19:15–20; 22:8), all people were treated equally (Lev. 19: 33–34; Deut. 24:17–22), and no one was cheated (Lev. 19:35–36; Deut. 25:13–16)? This is not the UN's declaration of human rights from the twentieth century, but laws that are over 3,000 years old. No wonder Oxford scholar Christopher Wright says of these laws:

> Many Christians say they are inspired by the teaching of the Sermon on the Mount. Few of us have yet begun to live by the values of this "sermon" on Mount Sinai, when we seriously reflect on the implications of this chapter [in Leviticus].
>
> Wright, "Leviticus," 52

Jesus would later call the love of God and neighbor "the summary of all the law and the prophets." It is not hard to see the connection between a false creation of a god and relating to neighbors. A walk through most Christian bookshops confirms that the temptation to make a god out of our own desires is still alive and well. "You can justify buying anything you want," they seem to say, "because a god wants you to be happy." The idols of this age say you can buy meaning in life in a department store, while the real God weeps that his creation has swallowed such delusions whole without chewing, and longs for us to love our neighbor in need.

The starving millions have no voice against the shrieks of temporal happiness, for which those pursuing such things risk all. Authentic loving of God and neighbor, then, is still the great need of the hour.

No sooner had the Lord outlined these laws to Moses than did the reality hit that people would break them. When Moses descended the mountain, his face literally shining after talking with the living God, he saw Aaron. Aaron had led the newly liberated people in worship of a golden calf. They had made a massive effort to collect gold, melt it down, and hand it to a new elite minority to create a calf. They wanted a "god" that they could handle and get to do whatever they wanted. Everything the Egyptians had done to them was now being attempted with each other and the god at the bottom of Mount Sinai.

It would take forty years of wandering around in the desert to make the Hebrew people ready to enter the Promised Land, free of internalized Egyptian oppression. There was so much oppression internalized in them that needed to be dried out before they could be the nation God wanted them to be.

Once the Hebrews entered the Promised Land, the struggle to be faithful to God and his commandments, expectations, and agreements became the story of the Hebrew Bible. God gave new laws, providing the basic expectations of loving God and neighbor, but living by them beyond self-interests required a new spirit.

The Jubilee Laws as an Example of the Protection of the Weakest

In light of the above, let's consider the meaning of the jubilee laws. The word "jubilee" is a play on the Hebrew words for "joy" and "jubilation," and has a related word meaning of the "ram's horn trumpeting." This wordplay demonstrates what happened at the start of the fiftieth year, the jubilee year (after seven cycles of seven years). A blast from a ram's horn on the Day of Atonement launched a year that called for joy, liberation, and ensuring that justice and loving mercy occurred.

I consider three aspects of the jubilee laws to be at the heart of issues of poverty and injustice today.

First, the laws assume poverty is a constant battle in a fallen world. Mistakes are made, people do wrong to others, and bad agricultural practice happens. Diligence, then, is required to ensure that the disparity between rich and poor does not blow out. People can sell the land they are responsible for and even their own labor if they begin to lose the battle economically, but this state of being is not allowed to be permanent. There is a safety net. Since everything belongs to the Lord, every fifty years all reverts back to an equal distribution of land and free labor, and a year-long party erupts where no one works! Talk about a year worth a "jubilant" celebration!

Today the gap between rich and poor is growing at a staggering rate. Yet, the idea of such jubilee interventions or any restrictions on a people's economic "growth" is considered almost a swear word. The assumption of this "growth equals well-being" dogma needs to be challenged. Having more does not mean having a more meaningful life. Economic survival of the fittest means few survive with real dignity and few are truly joyful. Therefore, allowing a few of the "fittest" to accumulate insane amounts of property, cash, and toys while most in the world struggle to "survive" in misery does not reflect God's will for the world. A regular redistribution of wealth, then, is a radical idea required again today.

Second, the jubilee laws battle with sustainable environmental and production issues. Leaving the land fallow for a whole year was a way of providing the land with much-needed rest and re-cuperation. More than once this text says that the land belongs to the Lord and not humans—people are just looking after it for him. Just as people are not slaves and need rest, so the land must not be a slave and needs rest. Indeed, the land is not a servant of humans, but a part of the Lord's created family.

We live in a world today where the tension between the desire to produce more wealth and the need to keep the environment healthy has become a frightening battle with no long-term winners. There are enough natural resources to go around, but not enough for all to have what most think they need. *The Melbourne Age* of 30 November 2002 reported, for example, that 62 percent of Australians surveyed felt that they couldn't afford to buy what they really needed. In fact, almost half of the richest households—with incomes over $70,000—agreed. The story began, "Is the Aussie worker nothing but a middle-class whiner?" It is hard not to answer in the affirmative.

Why would any nation leave the ground fallow and not work for a year when there is money to be made to get more of what is really needed? While the answer may not please economic rationalists, advertising executives, or "third way" politicians, God wants us to know that our life on earth together is about much more than what we consume. Creation is groaning, but it need not if we free it and each other from unsustainable and unrealistic expectations. "Party on" for a year!

Third, the jubilee laws battle for secure housing and labor. At their heart is a concern for all people to have a place to call home and a sustainable livelihood. For people to have dignity, there are some minimal standards. Without housing and employment, life can become a constant battle for survival. In our slum, for example, some people have a secure, long-term lease from the Port Authority, which owns the land. Others, however, do not have such security. It is no surprise which parts of the slum have the biggest drug, violence, and hygiene issues—the neighborhoods with the least secure housing. When you know you can have long-term security, you have greater power over your own circumstances, and this creates a better future.

Perhaps secure housing is one of the biggest issues facing a world with over one billion living in slum and squatter settlements. In *The Mystery of Capital: Why Capitalism Triumphs in the West and Fails Everywhere Else*, Hernando de Soto, an activist from Peru, writes:

> The words "international poverty" too easily bring to mind images of destitute beggars sleeping on the curbs of Calcutta and hungry African children starving in the sand. These scenes are of course real, and millions of our fellow human beings demand and deserve our help. Nevertheless, the grimmest picture of the Third World is not the most accurate. Worse, it draws attention away from the arduous achievements of those small entrepreneurs who have triumphed over every imaginable obstacle to create the greater part of the wealth of their society. A truer image would depict a man and woman who have painstakingly saved to construct a house for themselves and their children and who are creating enterprises where nobody imagined they could be built. I resent the characterization of such heroic entrepreneurs as contributors to the problem of global poverty. They are not the problem. They are the solution.
>
> De Soto, *The Mystery of Capital*, 35–37

De Soto goes on to show how $9.3 trillion of capital ("more than all foreign aid put together") is in fact owned by the poor, in terms of property and businesses. Because these resources are "unauthorized"—and almost impossible for the poor to authorize without years of bureaucratic and legal red tape—the poor cannot use their own assets properly. For example, gaining a bank loan to expand a business using a slum home as collateral is impossible. De Soto argues that providing and protecting property ownership of slum communities today would change the face of poverty tomorrow. This could be done, but those who could change this injustice also benefit from this arrangement. This is the kind of poverty most of the world faces, stripping the poor of what is rightfully theirs by not recognizing it or giving them authority for it. Certainly, the experience of the Hebrews would relate to this kind of oppression on a global scale.

Sustainable and meaningful work is essential for all humans. Perhaps the microenterprises that are sprouting up all over the developing world have picked this up. Dave and Kerri, friends working in the Suam Plu slum, have worked with their local community to develop a small business making cards and soap. It employs twenty women, and their lives are radically improved for this involvement. In Klong Toey, too, Anji has founded three collectives of women who make jewelry and handicrafts. This brings women together to enjoy each other's company rather than being isolated, creates a sense of pride in designing and making something beautiful, and, of course, helps bring in an income stream. There is a sense when you watch these women, often at the community center chatting away and threading beads, that real dignity is being returned to them.

The Hebrew laws show that vigilance is essential in the ongoing battle for a sustainable future together. It requires careful efforts and legal interventions and expectations. In many ways the second law of thermodynamics—that the universe is winding down—is at play here, requiring everyone to be ever vigilant in protecting everyone's dignity, all the time.

Isaiah the prophet longed for the day when the jubilee would be initiated, but we have no historical evidence that it was ever tried by the Hebrew people. As we can imagine only too well today, there were too many vested interests to allow debt to go unpaid. Jesus, however, said that the jubilee was fulfilled in him (Luke 4) and those anointed by the Holy Spirit. Jesus's presence gave the power to do what the jubilee laws could only point toward. The same anointing of the Spirit of Jesus can be on us to liberate and set free the oppressed.

Does the Bible Really Say Ending Poverty Is Futile?

Almost any discussion about poverty with middle-class Christians ends up with a grab for the proof text, "You always have the poor with you" (John 12:8). It is as if this quote says all there is to say about the futility of responding to poverty. "The Bible says it, I believe it, that settles it." They conclude that if the Bible says misery is inevitable, we can't do anything of value about it. But does this text really say that we should just focus on Jesus like the woman who anointed Jesus's head with expensive ointment, and shrug our shoulders about ending poverty?

This New Testament story is found in Matthew 26:6–13, but it is important that we remember the tradition from which this phrase Jesus quoted came: Deuteronomy and the Mosaic law we discussed above. Jesus did indeed quote in part the following text to Judas and the other disciples: "Since there will never cease to be some in need on the earth, I therefore command you, 'Open your hand to the poor and needy neighbor in your land'" (Deut. 15:11). For centuries this verse has been used to say that it is futile to respond to the poor and better to give to the church. Far from calling for passive acceptance of poverty, however, it calls for diligence and commitment to keep making poverty history, to keep opening our hand to the poor. (Again, it is worth reading each of the versions quietly a number of times over to see what most strikes you.)

First, the context of this story is clear. Jesus is in the home of Simon the leper in Bethany (Mark 14:3a). Lepers in those days were the most unclean of the unclean in society. It was thought that just by touching a leper you would catch the disease and need to be quarantined. Jesus broke ceremonial and hygiene laws just by being in such a person's home. So it's clear Jesus was hosted by a poor person who was well known enough to be named as Simon. Jesus risked his reputation and freedom to be present there that day.

Second, a woman, most probably a prostitute, poured out her expensive ointment on Jesus's head (Mark 14:3b). We can easily miss what happened here because it is so culturally loaded. The unraveled hair of a woman was only for a woman's husband. The feet were the lowest part of the body that no one but domestic help touched. The ointment was most probably a prostitute's most expensive possession and normally used as part of trade. So here we have a prostitute, one of society's most marginalized, giving her resources away to Jesus.

Third, Judas and the other disciples saw that this money, worth almost the salary of a laborer for a year, could be better used for the poor (Mark 14:4). In John's Gospel we're are tipped off about Judas's motivations: "He said this not because he cared about the poor, but because he was a thief; he kept the common purse and used to steal what was put into it" (John 12:6). Clearly, Judas wanted to use the prostitute's resources for himself. He was so blinded by greed that he couldn't see that a poor person was using her resources in another poor person's home!

Fourth, far from buying into the futility of poverty, Jesus used the symbolism of this woman's trade and transformed it. The woman gave Jesus what she had and anointed Jesus for his immenent burial. Jesus said that this poor lady made a historical contribution that would be talked about forever. Indeed, that witness includes this very moment as we consider what this story has to say about ending poverty. In a fallen world there will be those in need. That is no cause for giving up, however.

As the jubilee and other Hebrew laws reveal, we must be diligent to ensure that if anyone's dignity is lost, it is not lost for long. Jesus showed us this when he broke laws, allowing a woman to anoint his head with all she had to offer.

This story asks if we will be more like the leper and the prostitute and give everything we have to Jesus, or if we will make excuses and never get around to doing the right thing because of the voices that say there are better things to do for those who "deserve" it more.

Personal Reflection: Law Without Order

A group of brown-clothed police officers arrived at our neighborhood alleyways in April 2003—not good news. In fact, since a "war on drugs" had been pronounced by the Thai prime minister earlier that month, whenever the police came to a poor neighborhood like ours, it was potentially lethal. After a "blacklist" of 329,000 suspects was made, over 2,500 people were killed by the police and underworld figures. Few arrests were made in relation to these murders and "extrajudicial killings." Few "Mr. Bigs" of the drug world were caught—most of the people killed in this "war" were poor, including at least twelve from our community. Our neighbors had every right to go pale and protest their innocence in rapid-fire Thai and exuberant hand gestures as their gun-carrying guests silently made their way to the home of the next target, just a few doors down from our home.

Rather than the poor being protected by the law, in this case they were threatened by it. The theory was simple: drugs are bad, and a war is required—scour the nation and they will disappear. Since drugs are most prevalent in places of despair, the poor were most targeted. Few rich were affected.

The police eventually left our neighbor's home. They were still alive to talk to us about it. Apparently, the new concrete cladding they had just put up on the front of their home had raised suspicions. Where did they get the money for that? They must be selling drugs. Of course, no one bothered to find out that our neighbor's sister had married a German and had just sent money home to help fix up the house.

It was hard for us to know how to respond. The prime minister announced in December that the war on drugs had been won. However, when I first wrote about this in December 2003, the king of Thailand had just made his annual birthday speech, wanting to know who died and how, and who is being held responsible. All kinds of back flips emerged, including the number of dead going down by at least a thousand! We pray the law can be used to protect the most vulnerable rather than persecute them—even if they buy new concrete cladding!

In Springvale in 1998 I had a similar feeling about the futility of poverty and powerlessness. One of our neighbors had lost $8,000 at the new casino in Melbourne and had money lenders ringing him up and threatening him. Yet free buses picked up new patrons out of the front of our neighborhood welfare center and primary schools. The state premier in Victoria at that time, Jeff Kennett, had just announced that a "gambling-led recovery" was on its way now that a massive casino was being built and newly legalized poker machines were springing up all over the city. Who were we to take on big business and government? People have a right to gamble if they want. What could we do about it?

We had to find a way not to be neutral and try to find ways to restrain the powers that be. Rev. Tim Costello had initiated the Inter-Church Gambling Taskforce, and a colleague from UNOH and I went to see him to ask what we could do. He was very patient with our frustrations and ideas. "Perhaps super gluing shut the casino's ATMs might not be the most effective response," he advised.

What did work was that we got involved with a prayer vigil in front of the casino, developed some ideas on how to tighten legislation (including restricting advertising), and found ways to warn people of the addictive nature of gambling. It didn't feel like much, to be honest, in the face of such a monster, but at least it was something.

When the temporary casino was replaced with a new gas-fireball-breathing, laser-light shooting, permanent casino on the banks of the Yarra River, we decided to have a "Not the casino party" on the other side. Over 8,000 turned up to our party, including celebrities, comedians, and musicians. I was given the honor of going across the river in a boat and planting the Australian flag on the grass in front of the new casino. I can remember the PVC plastic pole bending and not quite getting into the hard turf as thousands cheered on the other side of the river. We reclaimed this land for the people!

Only two years later, what seemed like a futile attempt had gained momentum to such an extent that the premier—the most popular ever at the time of the casino opening—was ousted in an election. New laws regulating gaming came in with the new premier, who was surprised to win on the back of ordinary people reacting to the gambling-led recovery rhetoric.

Here in Bangkok it is hard not to be overwhelmed by the very physical needs of AIDS, housing security, and under- and unemployment. I think especially of two women who escaped from a brothel on the Thai border early in 2005. They were locked in a factory building and had only escaped by tricking a customer. Despite prostitution being illegal in Thailand, they said the police ran this brothel. Where is the law to protect the vulnerable and restrain the powerful?

Futility is never a good enough response in the face of poverty and injustice. If poverty is about abuse of power, then Jesus's example of standing with a leper in his home and encouraging a prostitute to make a historic contribution to the world rings in my ears. This solidarity gives hope that things don't have to be this way. Even when others try to distort God's image in people, lives can have dignity if Jesus's solidarity is followed. Perhaps we could do worse than celebrate a common jubilee-style redistribution of wealth and having a party, ready to fight poverty another day!

Challenge

Rather than accepting poverty, the biblical laws encouraged the Hebrew people to be diligent in ensuring that the weakest were not overcome by the most powerful. Are there ways that God is calling us to look at the causes of poverty and risk ourselves to strengthen those most vulnerable lives?

Questions for Discussion

- Which of the Hebrew laws that you read stood out as the one most worth trying again? Why?
- What do these laws reveal to you about responding to poverty?
- Discuss this statement: "'You always have the poor with you' is a challenge, not a given." Is this true or false? Why?
- Why are laws so important in combating poverty today?

A Personal Exercise

Think of the most vulnerable people you know. Who have the most power over these people and could abuse this power if they were not restrained? Come up with a law that, if enforced, could help protect these people and allow justice to happen.

Hebrew Poetry
and the Awesome Truth

Opening Reflection: The Truth Is Awfully Extreme!

I once heard a lecturer say, "The truth is always extreme." Hebrew poetry is a rich illustration of this. It was naming the awful truth about their collective life with God that sustained the Hebrew people, making a difference between despair and the hope to carry on as the vulnerabilities of life unfolded.

Hebrew leaders rose and fell, and after 200 years in the Promised Land, the Hebrew people established kings. This was an attempt to try to ward off attacks from their enemies and to consolidate their place in the world. With King Solomon in particular, the temple was founded, and this was a critical monument to national identity and faith.

With this concentration of power, it became harder to restrain the powerful. The excesses of life began to undermine faithfulness to the Lord and the reasons for the Hebrew people's liberation from Egypt. Ultimately, this led to exile. During this whole time, the Hebrews searched hard to find and express truth. God responded to this search and gave precious moments and insights that were shared communally. This was often recorded in the form of poetry, and three thousand years later it inspires Christians like few other kinds of biblical literature can.

Psalms and the "wisdom" literature (Job, Proverbs, and Ecclesiastes) are the prayers, poetry, sayings, and songs that express insights that emerged during the 400 years of the kings and into the nation's deportation from the Promised Land. So important were these insights into reality that when the capital, Jerusalem, fell in 587 BC and many Hebrews became displaced refugees, they used these insights to keep alive their faith in Yahweh. Indeed, as we will see, this literature has a special hope for those on the underside of history even today. (Try reading and praying aloud Psalm 77 as if you were a refugee, longing to be home but knowing that it is impossible for you right now.) Those who want to use it simply for the personal piety that is so common today are missing the point of it.

The Bible's Call: Keeping Hebrew Wisdom Poetry in Context

To keep these Hebrew texts in their context as we look at what they have to say about poverty and the awful truth, two principles need to be kept in mind.

First, truth is liberating only as far as it is recognized and acted on. The Hebrews did not consider "truth" as simply a true or false fact. Gaining control over a piece of information was not the same as gaining wisdom. The former is about mere facts—they might be correct facts in the broadest sense—whereas truth in the Hebrew sense recognizes a connection between people and the broader, timeless, outside world, and is experienced internally and personalized. Thus in Psalm 119 it is written, "Your law is the truth." (Here "law" refers to a code to live by, given by God to Moses.) This code is sound, it holds water, it endures, and is forever transformative if it is recognized and acted on. Such truth is about transformative insight into how to live right, rather than an answer to a scientific equation. Indeed, how could one measure the truth of a command or law? To recognize truth in this Hebrew sense, then, means to step out and act in ways consistent with God's character. Until then it is simply an idea or a thought or a fact that someone else considers important.

Second, we have the best opportunity of recognizing and acting on truth when we stand attentively in the presence of God. Even at our worst—and some psalms, particularly those attributed to King David, are putrid—the God of truth is there. The Lord is truth, and so it is from the Lord that all truth originates. The need to "meditate" and "be still" before the living God so that God can be heard above other voices, however, is not for the faint-hearted. This is not because God is not willing to speak, but because the more putrid our ways, the less we have the receptors to hear truth. This is what makes King David such an unusual character and makes his prayerful insights all the more remarkable. Fundamentally flawed, he abused power, had a person murdered, and raped a citizen. But David was still able to communicate with God. Indeed, God reached David, and David found responses that were real. These responses also resonated with others so much that they wanted to pray them, too. These poems and songs show both what is right and that God is the source of truth. Humans can respond, but it is God who gives such transformative insights.

The following passages are "samples" relating to poverty from the Hebrew poetry books. We cannot examine here every angle of every poem relating to poverty in these books. Instead, I have chosen a few passages from each book as representative of what Hebrew poetry has to say about making poverty personal.

There is a warning required for prayerfully reading Hebrew poetry. Allow yourself to hear these sample texts afresh, with a quiet heart and a willingness to act together with others, as the first readers did. If you are part of a small study group, please try to trust God's leading in your discussions, sit with the paradoxes the poetry raises, and, especially, don't attempt to water down poetic insights to make responses easier. Some of the ideas here are true for us today, no matter how extreme they may seem. If you can do this, you have a real opportunity to find the awful and awesome truth about us, our God, and poverty today!

Job: No Neutrality Regarding Who Suffers

Poverty can happen to anyone. This is the message of one of the most ancient books of poetry of the Hebrew Bible—Job. As a kid just learning to read I thought this book was about jobs— and the pain in getting one. Today, I'm not sure this quirk in translation is that far from the truth. This epic poem follows the job done on Job.

A central theme in Job is that if poverty can happen to someone like Job, then no one is immune. Job is described as "blameless" and "upright." These descriptions are not from his mother, but from the Lord. Yet, despite his upright character, Job is destined to suffer—painfully and undeservedly.

This possibility—becoming an innocent victim of poverty—is a distinctly Judeo-Christian view. For example, in animistic and karmic-based religions, everyone gets what they deserve. Disabled, no job, no children—these are the consequences of not doing enough of the right things—or too much of the wrong things—in this life or the last. In a karmic world view the answer is to take some personal responsibility for poverty and suffering. Suck it up now so it doesn't happen again.

Reflect on Job 19:7–29 as the cry of an innocent man facing poverty: "Even when I cry out, 'Violence!' I am not answered; I call aloud, but there is no justice. He has walled up my way."

What is remarkable about Job is that as he bears this suffering, he still has a future hope, and is not crushed by despair. "For I know that my Redeemer lives, and at the last he will stand upon the earth; and after my skin has been thus destroyed, then in my flesh I shall see God, whom I shall see on my side." As Christians, it is hard not to read here the hope of Christ, who is the God who "stands upon the earth" and stands on the side of the poor. Even if Job may not see this hope while he is alive, he knows justice will come and that it is better to be dead and just than alive and oppressing.

I often see the courage of Job today. There are those who have not internalized the lies of a society that, like Job's attendants, wants them to blame themselves. I think especially of the Burmese National League for Democracy leaders. They meet and try as best they can to act as the legitimate government of Burma— they won the election in 1990—but power was never handed on. As exiles in their own land or in jungles or in harsh jails, they are labeled terrorists by the military junta. They are called illegal fugitives and traitors, but these NLD leaders know the truth of who they really are—the ones who justice and history will one day say were in the right.

The Psalms: No Neutrality in Judgment

The Psalms teach us to pray not with pious pleasantries and religious clichés, but with raw honesty. Sometimes furious or despairing, yet somehow always hopeful in the presence of the Lord, the Psalms emerged as a way for Hebrews to sing collectively before God about what was really happening. Insight and actions resulted.

The Psalms were written by many writers as poetry to be sung in community, not as doctrinal treatises or sermons to be adhered to. A particular literary rhythm is often used here. It is called parallelism: saying the same thing twice with different words, creating a richer insight and rhythm. An example of this is Psalm 35:10:

> All my bones shall say,
> "O LORD, who is like you?
> You deliver the weak from those too strong for them,
> the weak and needy from those who despoil them."

Deliverance for those who are not strong enough to do it by themselves is the theme here. The psalmist can feel it in his bones. The Lord's very character is just, and therefore the Lord liberates the needy and weak from the strong and those who despoil them. The two lines express this one truth. Unlike poetic devices such as rhyming, these kinds of rhythms survive translation. If they only rhymed in Hebrew, then when translated into other languages they would not be understandable. It is as if God chose a universal form of poetry to express his angst, passion, and hope.

The richness of this kind of poetry and its relationship to poverty can be seen in the theme of judgment in the Psalms. This theme seems almost fundamentalist to our modern ears and is easily avoided for more politically correct and comforting prayers. Yet, truth and right judgment make all the difference to the poor, then and now. In fact, hardly a psalm avoids the idea of judgment.

Judgment in the Psalms is always good news—if you are poor or powerless. Most justice systems throughout the ages have been corruptible and least accessible to the poor. Even in modern Western democracies, the more money you have, the better your opportunity for justice, no matter what you are accused of. Justice might be blind, but if you can afford the best advocates that money can buy, she is not deaf.

Of course, in 500 BC the "little people" of society were not heard at all, no matter how watertight their case. In the Psalms the "courts" almost always speak of what we would call civil, not criminal, cases. A person would bring a case to the temple against another person for a judgment and restitution rather than seeking a pardon or guilty verdict. A just judge would then right the wrongs.

Psalm 82 is an example of this judgment theme. In its historical context of the poor not being heard, this text is dynamite—it takes a clear shot at those judges who should have championed the poor, ensuring their rights were upheld, but who took bribes from the rich:

God has taken his place in the divine council;
    in the midst of the gods he holds judgment:
"How long will you judge unjustly
    and show partiality to the wicked?
Give justice to the weak and the orphan;
    maintain the right of the lowly and the destitute.
Rescue the weak and the needy;
    deliver them from the hand of the wicked."
They have neither knowledge nor understanding,
    they walk around in darkness;
    all the foundations of the earth are shaken.
I say, "You are gods,
    children of the Most High, all of you;
    nevertheless, you shall die like mortals,
    and fall like any prince."
Rise up, O God, judge the earth;
    for all the nations belong to you!

There is a comparison here between the God of Israel and other leaders ("gods"). As the highest authority, the Lord expects those who have power—whether inside or outside Israel—to be instruments of justice and to right wrongs. God will do this and commands those who are in power to do this without delay. The cry at the end is that God will "rise up" to bring justice quickly, even if rulers don't.

There is an interesting parallelism here. The terms "just" and "right" are often paired together in the Hebrew Bible. In Hebrew the terms are *mishpat* and *sedakah,* and they always relate to the provision of social justice for those groups in society who are poor or marginalized in any way. Those named in this text are those who are poor, needy, orphaned, or widowed—the ones who are not generally given access to just and fair judgments and restitution. In this sense the Bible always talks about "doing justice," rather than "getting justice," as it is always about the positive action of restitution.

There is extreme language in this psalm with which few of us are comfortable. Those who oppress the poor are "wicked" and are wished dead. If they don't stand with the poor "they have neither knowledge nor understanding, they walk around in darkness;

all the foundations of the earth are shaken." A kind of curse is wished on them. This is not uncommon in the Psalms. The term "enemy" is used fifty-nine times. For example, in Psalm 68:1–2 there is the prayer, "Let God rise up, let his enemies be scattered; let those who hate him flee before him. As smoke is driven away, so drive them away; as wax melts before the fire, let the wicked perish before God." Few of us, even at our most vicious, would wish those we don't like to melt like wax. Talk about poetic justice! Even the most horrendous Tarantino revenge movies could hardly compete with this prayer.

What do we do with this raw emotion? Stoke up the bonfires for the rich and powerful or others we don't like? Many a movement has created commitment through expressing angst and then enacting revenge on those it sees as enemies, thinking that exterminating them will alleviate their suffering.

While in 500 BC the ways that wrongs could be righted were limited—there was no penal system, for example—I don't think that this is what the psalmists are saying to God. C. S. Lewis once wrote of the prayerful cursing in the Psalms in a way that I think can help our understanding of these texts:

> If the Jews cursed more bitterly than the Pagans this was, I think, at least in part because they took right and wrong more seriously. For if we look at their railings we find they were usually angry not simply because things have been done to them, but because these things are manifestly wrong [and] are hateful to God as well as to the victim. . . . The Jews sinned in this matter worse than the Pagans not because they were further from God but because they were nearer to him. For the Supernatural, entering a human soul opens it to new possibilities of both good and evil. From that point the road branches, one to sanctity, love, humility, the other to spiritual pride, self-righteousness, persecuting zeal. And no way back to the mere humdrum virtues and vices of the unawakened soul. If the Divine call does not make us better, it will make us very much worse. Of all bad men religious bad men are the worst. Of all created beings the wickedest is the one who originally stood in the immediate presence of God. There seems

no way out of this. It gives a new application to our Lord's words about "counting the cost."

Lewis, *Reflections on the Psalms*, 31–32

What was a normal and balanced position in society—denying justice to the poor—is in the presence of God a most heinous crime that should make our emotions boil over. Perhaps the fear of becoming "extremists" is most real if we get even a slight glimpse of the way God sees the world. Certainly we have to be prepared to be passionate and out of step with our contemporaries to see the world in such terms, prepared to feel the injustices of the poor "deep in our bones."

Cursing to God the powerful people who oppress the poor, as the psalmists often do, seems to be a little-practiced sin today. Most Christians simply can't see how wrong and horrendous such acts of oppression are, let alone feel strongly enough to swear to God about it and take sides. Seriously, when was the last time you heard someone get up in a church service and start shouting to God, "Rise up, exterminate those bastards who lock up asylum seekers to stay in sweet with military dictators"? Yet, if Psalm 82 says anything, it is that God is not neutral on issues of oppression towards the poor, and taking sides emotionally and practically is required by his people, particularly those who have some power to right wrongs.

Proverbs: No Neutrality with People

I have noticed lately that the only places I hear Proverbs quoted is by prosperity preachers or in cute greeting cards. Few others seem to love or even know what to do with this collection of sayings attributed to King Solomon. Yet, what Proverbs has to say about poverty would please neither.

As you may remember, Solomon was the third Hebrew king, was responsible for building the temple, and had thousands of wives and concubines. Perhaps there is some common ground

with prosperity preachers and greeting-card multinationals here—
at least with the building of enormous temples that would put a
smile on Freud's face!

In reflecting on the nature of poverty today in Proverbs, we
do have problems. What do we do with texts that say, "The LORD
does not let the righteous go hungry, but he thwarts the craving
of the wicked. A slack hand causes poverty, but the hand of the
diligent makes rich" (Prov. 10:3–4)?

Are we content to blame the poor for being slack and not being
righteous enough, or assert that the rich are only rich because they
are diligent? Some Christians are content to live their lives by such
notions—but obviously only the ones who are not poor!

It is a dangerous thing, however, to claim worthiness above
those who are hungry. In fact, it is impossible to do if you are to
avoid being "self-righteous." Before I respond to what these kinds
of proverbs are talking about and their relevance for today, let's
look at a few other proverbs that would not make rich Christians
feel so smug:

> "The field of the poor may yield much food, but it is swept away
> through injustice." (13:23)

> "Those who oppress the poor insult their Maker, but those who
> are kind to the needy honor him." (14:31)

> "It is better to be of a lowly spirit among the poor than to divide
> the spoil with the proud." (16:19)

> "Better the poor walking in integrity than one perverse of speech
> who is a fool." (19:1)

> "If you close your ear to the cry of the poor, you will cry out and
> not be heard." (21:13)

I don't think these proverbs have ever been engraved on com-
plimentary "golden eagles" given away to those who donate to
televangelists' ministries.

Proverbs 22 is worth closer reflection here. It should be read the whole way through, but here are some key verses that go to the heart of what it means to be poor and the responsibilities we have not even to associate with powerful people who exploit the poor, never mind claim our own righteousness.

> A good name is to be chosen rather than great riches,
>   and favor is better than silver or gold.
> The rich and the poor have this in common:
>   the LORD is the maker of them all.
> The clever see danger and hide;
>   but the simple go on, and suffer for it.
> The reward for humility and fear of the LORD
>   is riches and honor and life.
> Thorns and snares are in the way of the perverse;
>   the cautious will keep far from them.
> Train children in the right way,
>   and when old, they will not stray.
> The rich rule over the poor,
>   and the borrower is the slave of the lender.
> Whoever sows injustice will reap calamity,
>   and the rod of anger will fail.
> Those who are generous are blessed,
>   for they share their bread with the poor.
> Drive out a scoffer, and strife goes out;
>   quarrelling and abuse will cease.
> Those who love a pure heart and are gracious in speech
>   will have the king as a friend.
> The eyes of the LORD keep watch over knowledge,
>   but he overthrows the words of the faithless.
> The lazy person says, "There is a lion outside!
>   I shall be killed in the streets!"
> The mouth of a loose woman is a deep pit;
>   he with whom the LORD is angry falls into it.
> Folly is bound up in the heart of a boy,
>   but the rod of discipline drives it far away.
> Oppressing the poor in order to enrich oneself,
>   and giving to the rich, will lead only to loss.
> The words of the wise:

Incline your ear and hear my words,
    and apply your mind to my teaching;
    for it will be pleasant if you keep them within you,
    if all of them are ready on your lips.
So that your trust may be in the LORD,
    I have made them known to you today—yes, to you.
Have I not written for you thirty sayings
    of admonition and knowledge,
    to show you what is right and true,
    so that you may give a true answer
    to those who sent you?
Do not rob the poor because they are poor,
    or crush the afflicted at the gate;
    for the LORD pleads their cause
    and despoils of life those who despoil them.
Make no friends with those given to anger,
    and do not associate with hotheads,
    or you may learn their ways and
    entangle yourself in a snare.
Do not be one of those who give pledges,
    who become surety for debts.
If you have nothing with which to pay,
    why should your bed be taken from under you?
Do not remove the ancient landmark
    that your ancestors set up.
Do you see those who are skilful in their work?
    They will serve kings;
    they will not serve common people.

Many scholars consider King Solomon's reign to be the beginning of the end for the Hebrew people. His opulent lifestyle and concentration of power undermined the revolutionary movement from Egypt and the code given to Moses by God. It could even be said that Solomon represents in many ways what Egypt stood for—he was proud, exploitative, and built huge monuments. Yet, God used this flawed man and his insights to build the temple to the glory of God, and thereby touched lives.

Solomon's insights on poverty do seem paradoxical. At some points he scolded those who made money by exploiting the poor, warning readers from even being friends with such people. Yet, in this same chapter he returns to the theme of everything really coming from God and wealth being a sign of God's blessing. In a time when there was no welfare safety net, the warnings of the need for responsibility should have been heard as life-giving insights, not as judgments on the poor. We will reflect further on the nature of blessing in the New Testament in later chapters, but it is enough for now to say that this notion of blessing as deserved wealth is indeed here, even if it is "weighed up" against the practical notion of judgments about how wealth is obtained.

Ecclesiastes: No Neutrality in Exploitation

If Proverbs is quoted in a meaningful way rarely today, then few know what to make of Ecclesiastes. Whether liberal or conservative, this book seems to offer little wisdom to share. Perhaps it is best known for its verses about "every season," which were made into a popular song in the 1960s and used in the soundtrack of the movie *Forrest Gump*. Yet, this poem contains one of the most brutal critiques of the exploitative powers of worker-capital relationships ever written. It makes Marx look like Ronald Reagan's friend! The theme of poverty as the exploitative use of power occurs throughout the Hebrew scriptures, starting with the Hebrews' slavery in Egypt (Exod. 1:11), and ending with the prophets' promises and curses about exploiting workers (Isa. 58:3; Mal. 3:5) and those who are marginalized in society, such as widows, orphans, and refugees (Jer. 7:5–7). In the New Testament the epistle of James explodes with criticism of exploitation and oppression to such a degree that the Christian faith and the exploitation of workers for gain are mutually incompatible (James 2–3). So the following text is a strong variation on a theme, and is worth prayerful consideration at a time where our labor rights and fair trade practices are vulnerable all over the world:

Again I saw all the oppressions that are practiced under the sun. Look, the tears of the oppressed—with no one to comfort them! On the side of their oppressors there was power—with no one to comfort them. And I thought the dead, who have already died, more fortunate than the living, who are still alive; but better than both is the one who has not yet been, and has not seen the evil deeds that are done under the sun.

Eccles. 4:1–3

Here, in clear and concise terms, the wise teacher in Ecclesiastes names the pain and the relationships that cause suffering and poverty. The oppressed have tears of agony and no power or authority to choose how they live their own lives. The oppressors have the power to exploit these workers, and yet they have no real comfort in themselves. Both sides of the conflict are miserable. In fact, so dark is this conflict that the wise teacher thinks that if both sides could see the truth of their situation, they would rather be dead than live with themselves.

Many today would prefer not to know that workers chained to sewing machines earn less than a dollar a day generating fashion clothing for the rich minority around the world. However awful, it is a reality nonetheless.

One of the central messages of Ecclesiastes, by contrast, is that life needs to be lived fully, free of expectations and the "evil deeds" of oppression and exploitation. "This is what I have seen to be good: it is fitting to eat and drink and find enjoyment in all the toil with which one toils under the sun the few days of the life God gives us: for this is our lot" (Eccles. 5:18). To try to make the most of a bad situation, to be engaged in the awful truths of life and savor each moment of life we have—this is good advice in such times. "Whatever your hand finds to do, do with your might" (Eccles. 9:10). This idea stands in stark contrast to those who flee from even thinking about difficult realities, trying to live in fantasy and illusion. Escape is not possible from this life. We must find ways of engaging with the truths we find ourselves faced with.

Song of Solomon: Sex and Poverty

What do we make of the erotic poetry of Song of Solomon? This is the only book in the Bible with no explicit mention of God or poverty, but it does have lots of explicit sex! If Ecclesiastes encourages a kind of reckless abandonment to life, then the Song of Solomon seems to be a love song about abandonment to sexual ecstasy.

The pet names used in the poem such as, "Your nose is like a tower of Lebanon," or, "Your teeth are like a flock of ewes" are unlikely turn-ons today! Yet, even in this poem there is a thread of wisdom for understanding poverty and life today. Almost certainly an early Hebrew wedding poem, there is a strong message outlining the importance of love, intimacy, and fidelity in relationships, especially between husband and wife. Without these relationships any person, or even a whole society, would be in trouble. An example of this theme is found in 2:4–7:

> He brought me to the banqueting house,
>   and his intention toward me was love.
> Sustain me with raisins,
>   refresh me with apples;
>   for I am faint with love.
> O that his left hand were under my head,
>   and that his right hand embraced me!
> I adjure you, O daughters of Jerusalem,
>   by the gazelles or the wild does:
>   do not stir up or awaken love until it is ready!

There is a security here that speaks of intimate love and seeking the best for a lover. This is something that poverty strips from families, and married couples in particular. Anthropologists such as Oscar Lewis have found that where there is poverty and injustice, domestic violence is soon found. It is as if poverty emasculates a man, and he seeks to prove his masculinity in unhealthy and often violent ways to those over whom he can have power. What we do not see in the Song of Solomon, by contrast, is a man trying to prove his masculinity because he feels socially

78

castrated. He can offer a banquet that includes raisins and apples (which seem to be some kind of aphrodisiac). Such an image is a long way from the bruises and secrets that haunt the lives of too many women and men in poverty. It is, however, an image of what God intends relationships between husband and wife to be like: intimate, celebratory, deeply loving. Can the poor be free to experience these kinds of relationships?

Personal Reflection: Confronting the Awful Truth, Hebrew-poetry Style

In late October 2003 I first brought our newborn baby Aiden out into the bright sunshine of our neighborhood courtyard. Sitting on the wooden bench seat in front of a cooking stall, I held Aiden in my arms, crowded in on all sides by neighborhood children and adults, each taking turns to say, "*Ja aire*" ("peek-a-boo"). My boy looked out through his big, blinking, blue eyes and seemed to emanate a kind of serenity that soothed even the most troubled of us. This sense of serenity seemed another world away from the dramas of the previous nine months.

There was no easy birth for Aiden. Doctors had told us that it was impossible for us to conceive a week before we did, Anji was bitten on the stomach by a centipede a month before the birth, and minutes after his birth Anji needed an operation to remove the placenta. If God has his hand on our lives from the foundation of the world, then Aiden must have fingerprint marks somewhere.

Yet there was one moment in the pregnancy that was so desperate that it made me pray a psalm like I have never before. The psalm was Psalm 22:1–2: "My God, my God, why have you forsaken me? Why are you so far from helping me, from the words of my groaning? O my God, I cry by day, but you do not answer; and by night, but find no rest."

Anji had received a phone call from her doctor. "Your baby has tested positive for Down syndrome." We were stunned. Of course, in the back of our minds we knew this was possible, but we hadn't really considered or verbalized it, or considered the implications. In a religious climate where disability is viewed as your karma, our baby (and/or us as parents) would be thought to have done something terrible to deserve this. The Crew Duen, the principal of the preschool at our community center here, has a daughter with Down syndrome. Our hearts had broken over the lack of compassion and services, and also the deep prejudices, little Em and her family had to face.

Could we put our baby through all that if we didn't have to? That morning, in an instant, our vocation in Bangkok, coupled with some urgent needs in UNOH Melbourne, seemed to punch us in the stomach, wind us, and leave us lying on the ground.

Before we went to see the doctor and get further tests, I sent an e-mail to a friend and mentor, Ian Corlett, asking for his prayers and advice. His adopted daughter Beck, his pride and joy—"his angel," he would often call her—suffered from Down syndrome. Ian rang us up immediately, and his solidarity and assurances that God was with us whatever happened were a kind of grace that touched us, providing what we needed to keep going.

Deep within I began to know that we could trust God in all this, and that he knew what kind of baby we would have when he had called us to Klong Toey. Perhaps being prepared to stay would be part of making life better for those with disabilities. Surely the few of us in this slum who believe the Bible, which includes the story of Job suffering undeservedly, had something to contribute. Like any vocation, the reasons why we start out and reasons why we stay do change as the costs unfold.

I continued to read Psalm 22:

> Yet, it was you who took me from the womb;
>   you kept me safe on my mother's breast.
> On you I was cast from my birth,
>   and since my mother bore me you have been my God.
> Do not be far from me, for trouble is near
>   and there is no one to help.

> Psalm 22:9–11

Our own powerlessness pointed us back to God. To be honest, we had little choice. In the midst of darkness, if we could only find a small amount of faith, faith as small as a mustard seed, it would be enough hope to hang on. Deep within, our Lord is the only one who can help because he knows deeply what suffering is, even from his own birth. Dorothy Day once said,

> We are told to put on Christ, and we think of him in his private life, his life of work, his public life, his teaching and his suffering life. But we do not think enough of his life as a little child, as a baby. His helplessness. His powerlessness. We have to be content to be in that state too. Not to be able to do anything, to accomplish anything.
>
> Day, *By Little and by Little*, 113

Many consider the torture of the cross to be depicted prophetically in Psalm 22. Jesus, of course, uttered the first lines, "My God, my God, why have you forsaken me?" while on the cross. This feeling of Godforsakenness is part of the call of obedience. Like Job, Jesus was willing to follow the Father's will even if he couldn't feel and see the evidence of the closeness.

In an amazing turn of events, Aiden ended up free of Down syndrome and the situation in Melbourne was resolved. Life does not always work out for the best, but sometimes if we trust and cry out like the psalmist in the dark times, we get the chance to hold our healthy babies in the sunshine. I doubt I have ever been more grateful for God's interventions and grace than that day in our courtyard.

Challenge

We often engage God only with our minds. What Hebrew poetry does is to engage our emotions in community prayer. It spares no feelings in expressing the truth of a situation. For when we can name a truth before God and others, we can own it and seek authentic liberation.

Questions for Discussion

- Which Bible verses in this chapter most challenged you about making poverty personal? Why?
- Compare and contrast Hebrew poetry with your experiences of contemporary worship. How are they different/similar?
- Discuss this statement: "God uses good and bad people to express truth. All truth, though, belongs to God." Do you agree or disagree? Why? Why not?
- What have been your most intimate experiences of God that included suffering? Why do suffering and prayer often go together?

A Personal Exercise

Ask a person you know who is facing poverty to help you write out a prayer to God. What would they want to say to God if they could say anything? Let them brainstorm as much or as little as they like. With their permission, try to write a contemporary psalm with parallelisms and the feelings and ideas from this person. Share the psalm with your friend facing poverty.

4

Prophetic Ministry—
Radical Hope
from the Margins

Opening Reflection: Recovering the Radical

The term "radical" is out of vogue these days. For many the term conjures up images of the 1970s—hairy and intense men (and some women), placard in one hand and bag of heavy books slung over a shoulder on their way to yet another protest march. For others it may convey outlaw, even fanatical, behavior. Few Christians want to be radical like that today.

Yet, the idea of being radical needs to be redeemed. Surely, it's a real alternative to today's polarities of "conservatives" and "liberals." "Radical" literally means "going to the roots." So perhaps we need to put fashion aside and resurrect this idea as we search to be both faithful to the roots of and reasons for our faith tradition (so-called conservative concerns) and relevant to the roots of and reasons for our current world crisis (so-called liberal concerns). In a world of so much poverty, it's time to put the old "culture wars" aside and sincerely seek to be both radically faithful to God and radically relevant to our world. This was the way and concern of the best of the Hebrew prophets, priests, and kings.

Whereas we saw the poetry and power of kings and sages in our previous chapters, in the prophets we see the lengths to which they went in order to offer radical hope. As we shall see, this hope was not just talked about, but also acted on by the prophets. They were the original radicals, living symbols of what was required to be both faithful to God and relevant to their times. If we are to take seriously the search for radical faithfulness and relevance in a world of so much poverty, perhaps the Hebrew prophets have much to teach us. They so often named the reality of the nations and the individuals they faced, touched again and again on the reason why the Hebrew people existed, and personally gave all they had to right the sometimes huge gap between these two concerns. This is the story of the relationship between the prophets and the Hebrew people.

While renewal may have started with the Bible's wild ones, it was only actualized when a partnership between the margins (the prophets) and the center (kings and priests) occurred. The center's willingness to give up privileges and not only listen, but also give all they had, to the alternate visions named by the edges, created real change. Why are the margins so important to the renewal of societies? Put simply, the marginalized are the litmus test of whether the ideals and values of a society are working or not. The center may at best see the overall picture and be ready to respond, but the margins live the failures of that picture. If Hebrew history offers anything today in our struggle against stubborn poverty, perhaps it is that when the center does not listen to the margins, there is a spiraling and tragic decline of both center-leaders and the nation as a whole. The requirement of solidarity between wild edges and the established center is something faith communities, organizations, and governments today need to hear again and again. It is especially important if we are to end oppression of the margins by the center. Freedom from oppression requires changes by the powerful center, not just by the margins.

The Bible's Call: David and Nathan

An example of the kind of relationship that worked for radical change is the story of King David and the prophet Nathan. David was arguably the greatest Hebrew king of all time. He had established the capital, Jerusalem, brought all the Hebrew tribes together, and was a "man after God's own heart." The prophet Nathan had been involved early in David's ministry, prophesying future divine blessing of David's reign (2 Sam. 7:8–16). Yet, David later used his power to oppress a poor family. David had seduced—if not raped—a married woman named Bathsheba. He then gave orders to have her husband killed in battle. Bathsheba was pregnant with David's child.

After some time, Nathan plucked up the courage to face the most powerful king in Hebrew history (2 Sam. 11:27). What could he do? How could someone on the edges of power create any awareness and change?

(How do we help today's powerful people to know God and to act justly? Prayerfully take some time to read 2 Samuel 12:1–13 and reflect on the ways Nathan tried to do this and how David responded. How is this similar to or different from your experiences in confronting the abuses of power?)

Nathan had a deep love for both his nation and for David. He had access to the king and had journeyed with David over many years. His compassion required that he criticize and rebuke a friend, with all the risks that this represented. Many kings—including David—have had people stand up to them only to have them killed for far less. Yet, despite the risks, Nathan stood in solidarity with a poor family in crisis because he knew that this was what God required.

Nathan wasn't just being critical from a distance, throwing bricks over an ideological fence. The prophetic task is not just to be critical of those who are not on our side. That would just be propaganda, setting up "straw men" to strengthen "our side's" position by weakening theirs. To be critical of the ones we deeply love—those on our side—however, is the heart of the prophetic task, one that requires courage and compassion of the highest order.

Nathan faced David personally—eyeball to eyeball—and found a way to be heard. The ability for a legitimate criticism to be heard was perhaps Nathan's greatest genius. He didn't just blurt out what was wrong and then run away. Nathan came close to David and told a parable—a kind of case study in injustice and oppression. A man had taken something precious from another because he had power, even though he didn't need what was taken. David could see this clearly as abuse and injustice, but as soon as he started to rant, Nathan intervened. "You are the man," he explained. The king was devastated by the truth of this and eventually found a way of deep repentance and restitution.

Three Prongs of Prophetic Ministry: Piercing the Heart of Poverty and Oppression

What Nathan did was typical of the prophetic task throughout the Hebrew Bible. Walter Brueggemann writes, "The task of the prophetic ministry is to nurture, nourish, and evoke a consciousness and perception alternative to the consciousness and perception of the dominant culture" (*The Prophetic Imagination*, 13). We need to cultivate this imagination today in every person, group, and system. What was so radical about the alternate, prophetic dream in the Bible? I see three prongs emerging from the edges, which are either embraced (resulting in renewal) or rejected (resulting in tragedy) by the center. These three prongs of the prophets are radical because they pierce through to the reasons why Yahweh liberated the Hebrew people from Egypt. They are also radical because they reach down deep to the underlying issues that faced God's people at the time. Together these three prongs have the potential to pierce the heart of the oppressor again today.

Critiquing: A radical knowledge of God and his will

David eventually came to know and understand God again when he saw clearly his own acts of injustice and sought repentance. Nathan could see what David had done wrong and helped David to see how serious it was. Psalm 51 is attributed to David after this meeting with Nathan and gives us some insight into the response and renewal that occurred:

> Have mercy on me, O God,
>   according to your steadfast love;
>   according to your abundant mercy
>   blot out my transgressions.
> Wash me thoroughly from my iniquity,
>   and cleanse me from my sin.
> For I know my transgressions,
>   and my sin is ever before me.
> Against you, you alone, have I sinned,
>   and done what is evil in your sight,
>   so that you are justified in your sentence
>   and blameless when you pass judgment.
> Indeed, I was born guilty,
>   a sinner when my mother conceived me.
> You desire truth in the inward being;
>   therefore teach me wisdom in my secret heart.
> Purge me with hyssop, and I shall be clean;
>   wash me, and I shall be whiter than snow.
> Let me hear joy and gladness;
>   let the bones that you have crushed rejoice.
> Hide your face from my sins,
>   and blot out all my iniquities.
> Create in me a clean heart, O God,
>   and put a new and right spirit within me.
> Do not cast me away from your presence,
>   and do not take your holy spirit from me.
> Restore to me the joy of your salvation,
>   and sustain in me a willing spirit.
> Then I will teach transgressors your ways,
>   and sinners will return to you.

Deliver me from bloodshed, O God,
    O God of my salvation,
    and my tongue will sing aloud of your deliverance.
O LORD, open my lips,
    and my mouth will declare your praise.
For you have no delight in sacrifice;
    if I were to give a burnt offering,
    you would not be pleased.
The sacrifice acceptable to God is a broken spirit;
    a broken and contrite heart,
    O God, you will not despise.
Do good to Zion in your good pleasure;
    rebuild the walls of Jerusalem,
    then you will delight in right sacrifices,
    in burnt offerings and whole burnt offerings;
    then bulls will be offered on your altar.

Over and over again prophets are raised up to link the knowledge
and worship of God with the doing of justice. Really to know God
is to engage with the Lord's compassion and justice. To fail to enter
into these characteristics of the Lord is to fail to know God. An
example of this is Jeremiah's account of King Jehoiakim of Judah:

Did not your father eat and drink and do justice and righ-
    teousness? Then it was well with him.
He judged the cause of the poor and the needy;
    then it was well.
    Is not this to know me?
    says the LORD.

                                        Jeremiah 22:15b–16

Oppression upon oppression, deceit upon deceit!
    They refuse to know me, says the LORD. . . .
Thus says the LORD: Do not let the wise boast in their wisdom,
do not let the mighty boast in their might, do not let the wealthy
boast in their wealth; but let those who boast boast in this, that
they understand and know me, that I am the LORD; I act with

steadfast love, justice, and righteousness in the earth, for in these things I delight, says the LORD.

Jeremiah 9:6, 23–24

Hosea had a similar prophecy:

Hear the word of the LORD, O people of Israel; for the LORD has an indictment against the inhabitants of the land.
There is no faithfulness or loyalty, and no knowledge of God in the land.
Swearing, lying, and murder, and stealing and adultery break out; bloodshed follows bloodshed.
Therefore the land mourns, and all who live in it languish; together with the wild animals and the birds of the air, even the fish of the sea are perishing.

Hosea 4:1–3

How do we know if we know God? These prophets explain that a key test is that we are aware of our own power, and that we connect with the Lord's passion and heartbeat for those with less power. We would be sure of knowing God if we did all we could to stand with the poor and alleviate the suffering of others, especially the most vulnerable. (This is not "works" as something due because of our faith, but grace as evidence of true faith.) But these prophetic verses go further than our concern for reformation. They go to the heart of the Hebrew revelation of God. They say that the Lord God, who can't be known through handmade stone and gold images—like the so called "gods" of other nations that the second commandment expressly prohibits—can be known through doing justice, compassion, and goodness.

Why is this so? Whenever we are in solidarity with the poor and do that which is in our power to do, we touch on the reasons the Hebrews were freed. The same God who heard the cries of the oppressed in Egypt and responded still hears and responds passionately to the cries of the oppressed. The Lord's people today can do no less if they are truly his.

It has been said that revolutions simply exchange one set of oppressors for another, that power corrupts, and absolute power corrupts absolutely. In many ways the Hebrew nation's development and David's rise to kingship follow this pattern. David grew up poor and knew firsthand what marginalization was like. Because he was formerly a shepherd working in the wilderness, his rise to power and oppression betrays his roots. Yet, for all the inevitability of betrayal that power brings, the hope offered in the Hebrew Bible is that some in power can and do listen to the margins. We can know God afresh and respond to the alternative reality personified on the edges if we have people like Nathan with us, who can critique what we are doing wrong, and if we are ready to listen and respond.

This is no easy task, and no Hebrew ruler did this perfectly. Yet, Hebrew kings were not like other rulers of the time. Israel's rulers were not considered gods or to have unlimited power. As Abraham Heschel notes, "From the beginning of the monarchy, the king was at any moment in peril of rebuke, even rejection, by the prophets, who reminded him that the king's sovereignty was not unlimited, that over the king's *mishpat* (justice) stood the *mishpat* of the Lord—an idea that frequently clashed with the exigencies of government" (*The Prophets*, 2:259). When Israel's kings were at their most faithful, there was actually a kind of separation of powers, as we would call it today. The true prophets were unlike the "yes men" employed by similar rulers—they were a check and balance to keep leaders and nations from straying from God's will and intentions. So, while it is normally and naturally impossible for power to be used well consistently, with openness to the God who speaks from the margins, all things are possible.

David was devastated by his own sin. He had oppressed rather than protected the vulnerable as was required by his mandate as king and a member of God's people. In fact, according to the law, David should have been stoned to death for adultery. Yet, he was pardoned and given a fresh chance. There are many of us who can relate to Nathan in this story—the wise and courageous

90

prophet challenging the status quo. Yet, the responsibility of power is something all of us must face.

Could we dare to say that today's Western Christians are most like David, in the sense that we often do not see our own complicity in oppression? Like David, are we too often self-absorbed or busy, and able to find a quick justification for any action? Sophisticated code words employed to protect our own power allow us to keep oppressing others without a second thought. If we talk about the protection of our own rights, our own family, or our own nation as first priorities, who would really challenge us? Never mind that what our generation calls rights, our great-grandparents called privileges.

David and Nathan could have conspired together to justify oppressive actions, but they didn't. Nathan helped David name the reality of what had happened and, through repentance, this reality of injustice was turned into a deep knowledge of God.

What can be justified as "good" is seldom the "right thing." It is an interesting quirk of the ancient Greek language of the New Testament that our English words for "just" and "right" are the same Greek word, *dike*. If we are to know God truly, we too must become aware of what is just and right. When we are tempted to misuse our resources and power to get things we don't really need, we need to have people who can help us see reality. Tragically, few of us allow a Nathan into our lives.

David's response is a good response to any abuse of power—small or large. David did not blame others. He did not justify his own goodness to tip the scales in his favor and outweigh this horrendous deed. He did not use Nathan as a scapegoat, finding in him faults to deflect his own. On the contrary, David allowed Nathan to help him name the reality of his action, and accepted the consequences. David then sought restitution, trying to right his wrongs and do those things for which God had designed him.

Do we have a Nathan in our lives? Someone to whom we give permission to speak into our lives—personally, organizationally, or in the context of our faith community? A real test of this is the way in which we go about making key decisions. For example, if we really feel deep in our bones that we should take a certain course of action, who is it to whom we can point as someone through whom God could say "no" to us, and to whom we would actually listen? Is our power so absolute that no one can really speak to our key decision-making processes unless they agree with us?

Perhaps the six words that most undermine any chance of Christian community today are, "God told me to move on." Obviously, those who are informed of such a decision can do little about it. Who are they to say God says differently? For this reason, this kind of statement is often an abuse of power. It is simply too convenient to get out when the going gets tough and blame God, who may or may not want the person to move on. Not being prepared to work through discernment with those who don't have the power to move out—or choose to use their power to commit to the community—makes real knowledge of God's will impossible. The relatively recent trend of Christian community merry-go-rounds, moving from community to community, unable to commit through tough times, is a tragedy for all. No Christian worker or church member is ever remembered for how they start. How people finish is what lives on in a community's mind. Uttering those six oppressive words to those with whom you are in solidarity can therefore undermine a decade of goodwill and hard work. Indeed, few Hebrew kings finished their lives and leadership well due to the fact that they allowed the voices on the margins to fade.

The relationship between the prophet and the king was also important. That Nathan confronted the king and lived showed his independence from the governing structures. He worked alongside the king, but had no vested interest in the job. The prophet was a check and balance for the one with power. David was expected to listen to what his friend and prophet had to say. Nathan could only do that by being recognized and by having the authority to play a role different from those who made his leadership work.

We need to find ways to encourage space for the medicine men and women among us. We have so much to learn from the way Nathan went about this role. "Never offend anyone . . .

unintentionally," seemed to be Nathan's motto. Nathan (and most Hebrew prophets) had the ability to be heard and create awareness, but this space to be heard was created by the king.

My temptation, when I feel the need to challenge someone—which if I'm honest is something I dread because of the risks involved—is to want to shake them and blurt out, "What on earth are you doing?" as soon as we sit down. I let things build up and then want to explode. Nathan didn't do this. He patiently found a way so that David could hear him.

At times prophets are less subtle in linking the truth about knowing God and doing justice. Amos comes to mind with his take-no-prisoners rant on some rich ladies:

> Hear this word, you cows of Bashan
>> who are on Mount Samaria,
>> who oppress the poor, who crush the needy,
>> who say to their husbands,
>> "Bring something to drink!"
> The Lord God has sworn by his holiness:
>> The time is surely coming upon you,
>> when they shall take you away with hooks,
>> even the last of you with fishhooks.
> Through breaches in the wall you shall leave,
>> each one straight ahead;
>> and you shall be flung out into Harmon,
>> says the Lord.
>
> Amos 4:1–3

I'm not sure how this prophecy would have been received at the ladies' coffee morning. Then again, I'm not sure Amos would have spared the worship leaders convention either:

> Take away from me the noise of your songs;
>> I will not listen to the melody of your harps.
> But let justice roll down like waters,
>> and righteousness like an everflowing stream.
>
> Amos 5:23–24

So, as we will see later in this chapter, the prophets sometimes had to spell out judgment and consequences. In this case, however, Nathan's criticism was heard because of his tact, and David's willingness to listen and be open to know God's will and the justice for which God longs.

Will those of us with power allow those without formal power the voice to help us live justly with others? Or will we ignore such people, or make them scapegoats? The deep repentance that David showed did not happen by accident. Will we risk our friendships and power to rebuke those we love, as Nathan did? It is through the dynamics of these relationships that we find a radical knowledge of God, which in turn can help to make poverty evaporate.

Warning! Radical justice is coming

Nathan, however, did not stop raising awareness and making the link between knowing the Lord and doing justice. Once David saw "he was the man," Nathan did not spare him the nature of the consequences of this oppression.

Change requires seeing the dangers to which one direction leads. Change comes from a willingness to see a need to go on another path. The Hebrew Bible is full of prophetic warnings about the consequences of oppressing. In 1 Kings 21, for example, King Ahab wanted to buy the vineyard of a neighbor named Naboth because it was geographically close to his own. Naboth would not agree, and said, "The LORD forbid that I should give you my ancestral inheritance" (1 Kings 21:3). Like a spoiled brat, Ahab went home to sulk. "He lay down on his bed, turned away his face, and would not eat" (1 Kings 21:4). After a while Jezebel, Ahab's wife, got sick of the king moping about. She found out that it was a Hebrew subject who was holding out on the king and decided to fix the situation. She wrote a letter and gave a royal seal in Ahab's name to the nobles in Naboth's city, and then set up a kangaroo court. Two "scoundrels" were organized to give false testimony, saying, "Naboth cursed God and the king" (1 Kings 21:13). At the gate of the city, reserved for protection and justice of the weakest

94

against the strongest, Naboth was sentenced to death by stoning for high treason and blasphemy.

The co-conspirators, the nobles, then got the message to Jezebel that Naboth was dead, and she in turn couldn't wait to tell Ahab that he could now get the land he wanted. The powerful had won again—Ahab grabbed the land as soon as he could. A legal system intended to provide justice for the weakest was used by the powerful for their own gain. Nobody was the wiser . . . except the Lord, who let Elijah know what had happened.

Elijah is, perhaps, the most mercurial of all the prophets. He could take on the prophets of Baal in a duel to call down fire to burn up a beef offering. Yet, he could also sulk in a cave moaning about the fact that he was the only prophet left, even when he knew there were at least 100 prophets that Obadiah had hidden. So, Elijah was an interesting choice to be an answer to oppression. This is what the Lord said to Elijah:

> Go down to meet King Ahab of Israel, who rules in Samaria; he is now in the vineyard of Naboth, where he has gone to take possession. You shall say to him, "Thus says the LORD: Have you killed, and also taken possession?" You shall say to him, "Thus says the LORD: In the place where dogs licked up the blood of Naboth, dogs will also lick up your blood."
>
> 1 Kings 21:18–19

Elijah did what the Lord asked. Although, when he did met Ahab, he didn't just relay the message word for word. God used Elijah's personality and passion to give the warning:

> Ahab said to Elijah, "Have you found me, O my enemy?" He answered, "I have found you. Because you have sold yourself to do what is evil in the sight of the LORD, I will bring disaster on you; I will consume you, and will cut off from Ahab every male, bond or free, in Israel; and I will make your house like the house of Jeroboam son of Nebat, and like the house of Baasha son of Ahijah, because you have provoked me to anger and have caused Israel to sin. Also concerning Jezebel the LORD said, 'The dogs

shall eat Jezebel within the bounds of Jezreel.' Anyone belonging to Ahab who dies in the city the dogs shall eat; and anyone of his who dies in the open country the birds of the air shall eat."

(Indeed, there was no one like Ahab, who sold himself to do what was evil in the sight of the Lord, urged on by his wife Jezebel. He acted most abominably in going after idols, as the Amorites had done, whom the Lord drove out before the Israelites.)

1 Kings 21:20–26

Not a subtle or pretty prophecy. It's more like a Stephen King short story than a nice sermon. Yet, this warning created change in Ahab's heart and changed his behavior. "When Ahab heard those words, he tore his clothes and put sackcloth over his bare flesh; he fasted, lay in the sackcloth, and went about dejectedly" (1 Kings 21:27).

After such oppression, many of us would love to see how the Stephen King-like prophecy would be fulfilled. Yet, just as David had been shown grace for his oppression, the Lord responded to Ahab's repentance.

Then the word of the Lord came to Elijah the Tishbite: "Have you seen how Ahab has humbled himself before me? Because he has humbled himself before me, I will not bring the disaster in his days; but in his son's days I will bring the disaster on his house."

1 Kings 21:28–29

I am not sure Ahab's sons would be so pleased about the reprieve, but the next verse does explain that "for three years Aram and Israel continued without war" (1 Kings 22:1). Change can come through warnings about the consequences, even for rulers known to be evil. Destiny is a strange beast—we do have opportunity to repent and change it if we take the warnings personally.

Not everyone took prophetic warnings seriously. The prophecies regarding the fate of Jezebel were in fact fulfilled: she was thrown from a tower and eaten up by dogs before she could be buried (2 Kings 9:31–37), and the unjust social institutions that allowed this to happen were destroyed, too. The judgment of the city of Sodom is often associated with its sexual sin, but it was actually destroyed after being warned for oppressing the poor.

> This was the guilt of your sister Sodom: she and her daughters had pride, excess of food, and prosperous ease, but did not aid the poor and needy. They were haughty, and did abominable things before me; therefore I removed them when I saw it.
>
> Ezekiel 16:49–50

Within a generation of this prophecy from Amos, the northern kingdom of Israel was completely wiped out. Again, mistreatment of those facing poverty was a warning no one could afford to ignore.

> Hear this, you that trample on the needy,
>> and bring to ruin the poor of the land,
> saying, "When will the new moon be over
>> so that we may sell grain;
> and the sabbath,
>> so that we may offer wheat for sale?
> We will make the ephah small and the shekel great,
>> and practice deceit with false balances,
> buying the poor for silver
>> and the needy for a pair of sandals,
>> and selling the sweepings of the wheat."
> The LORD has sworn by the pride of Jacob:
>> Surely I will never forget any of their deeds.
> Shall not the land tremble on this account,
>> and everyone mourn who lives in it,
> and all of it rise like the Nile,
>> and be tossed about and sink again,
>> like the Nile of Egypt?
> On that day, says the Lord God,
>> I will make the sun go down at noon,
>> and darken the earth in broad daylight.
> I will turn your feasts into mourning,
>> and all your songs into lamentation;

97

I will bring sackcloth on all loins,
    and baldness on every head;
I will make it like the mourning for an only son,
    and the end of it like a bitter day.
The time is surely coming, says the Lord God,
    when I will send a famine on the land;
not a famine of bread, or a thirst for water,
    but of hearing the words of the Lord.
They shall wander from sea to sea,
    and from north to east;
they shall run to and fro,
    seeking the word of the Lord,
    but they shall not find it.

Amos 8:4–12

The warnings about benefiting from injustice are clear. Yet, another's sin is always clearer to see than our own. Ronald Sider once wrote, "If one is a member of a privileged class that profits from structural evil, and if one does nothing to try to change things, he or she stands guilty before God. Social evil is just as displeasing to God as personal evil. And it is more subtle" (*Rich Christians in an Age of Hunger*, 128). What does this mean to those who are benefiting from the stealing of Aboriginal land, when there has been no remorse or restitution? What does it mean for those profiting from slavery or segregation or from the colonization of far-off lands? What about those who are employed by or who have shares in multinational corporations that exploit cheap labor markets in the developing world to sell back to the West and, when labor becomes more costly in that region, move production to somewhere cheaper to start over again? Are these any less oppressive than Jezebel and Ahab?

Warnings about injustices and oppression have been given by the prophets, and we should take heed of these warnings, too. God will vindicate the poor—that is certain—and we had better stop our oppressing and get our sackcloth and ashes ready, seeking the Lord's forgiveness before it is too late. I for one don't want to end up as doggy dinner.

Offering: The radical hope of shalom and the final day of justice

The prophets were not just challengers and scaremongers, however. They held out an alternate vision, a hope for the future that went to the heart of why the Hebrew people were freed from oppression. "The land of milk and honey" became known for having a sense of *shalom*, or "peace." Typical images of this alternate vision come from Isaiah:

> I will appoint Peace [*shalom*] as your overseer and Righteousness as your taskmaster. Violence shall no more be heard in your land.
>
> Isaiah 60:17b–18a

Within the prophetic tradition came the idea of the "day of the Lord." This was a concern for an ultimate day when all wrongs would be righted and peace would come. This begins much earlier than the prophets. In Genesis 18 God, the "Judge of all the earth," intervened against the unjust because he heard the cries of the oppressed and chose Israel to be the nation to achieve "righteousness and justice" (Gen. 18:19) among the nations. Moses became the first liberator of the Hebrews from Egypt and spoke of a land of milk and honey. Judges emerged as kinds of enforcers of justice for those oppressing Israel, and Deborah in particular cited a coming day when this justice would be complete. In the previous chapter, we also saw this theme of judgment in the Psalms, for example Psalm 62, where after citing injustices such as extortion, robbery, and riches, the Lord promises to "repay to all according to their work." However, the idea of the "day of the Lord," or the "day of *mishpat*" (justice or judgment), is taken up even more explicitly and passionately by the prophets as the final day of the Lord's justice.

Freedom from Affliction

The prophets' view of a future hope is multifaceted. It includes the following freedoms.

99

Freedom from oppression

The rich and powerful will not always be so. For those who oppress, the "day" will be terrible; for those who are oppressed and victims of injustice, the "day" means vindication and ultimate freedom. For example, Isaiah prophesies, "For the yoke of their burden, and the bar across their shoulders, the rod of their oppressor, you have broken as on the day of Midian" (Isa. 9:4). God's passions, desires, and concerns for true justice for all, made known through the law and prophets, will not be thwarted forever. There is a day coming when the tolerance of God ends, when oppressors get what they deserve, and the oppressed will be fully liberated. (See also Isa. 11:4; 44:26; 51:14; 65:22; Ezek. 34:27–28.)

Freedom from disease and sickness

One aspect of poverty that will be alleviated on "that day" is disease. Isaiah's vision of *shalom* therefore includes wholeness of body. For example, he prophesies: "On that day the deaf shall hear the words of a scroll, and out of their gloom and darkness the eyes of the blind shall see. The meek shall obtain fresh joy in the LORD, and the neediest people shall exult in the Holy One of Israel" (Isa. 29:18–19). Disability and sickness is part of the cycle of poverty. If you had sickness or disease in biblical times, you could not work or go to school; if you couldn't work, you couldn't get money for treatment, would likely get sicker, and you therefore would be less likely to get back to work or school again. Little has changed today: illness and disability not only disables people, but also marginalizes them socially. (See also Isa. 32:3–5; 35:5–6; 42:7–16; 61:1–3; 65:20.) The difference between then and now is that medical treatment is available for many fatal diseases today, but many of the poor are excluded from access to treatment. Millions die each year from preventable and curable illnesses such as diarrhea, tuberculosis, and malaria because they can't afford the medicines. The prophets hold out hope that a day will come when all people will be whole again, that all will have physical and emotional wellness.

Freedom from want

On "that day" there will be no poverty—everybody will have what they need to live fulfilling and meaningful lives. Jeremiah 31:12 gives this vision: "They shall come and sing aloud on the height of Zion, and they shall be radiant over the goodness of the LORD, over the grain, the wine, and the oil, and over the young of the flock and the herd; their life shall become like a watered garden, and they shall never languish again." How the poor of the world would love to be described as having lives like a well-watered garden, in which everyone has enough to live meaningful, joyous, and happy lives! (See also Isa. 9:3; 27:3; 32:2; 35:1–2; 49:9–10; 65:21; Ezek. 34:26; Joel 2:1–9; 2:24–26; 3:18; Amos 9:43; Zeph. 3:30.)

Freedom from death

Death itself is the greatest oppressor of human beings. With the fall of humanity, death became inevitable and final. Yet, on "that day" even death will be conquered. In Daniel, for example, we find:

> At that time Michael, the great prince, the protector of your people, shall arise. There shall be a time of anguish, such as has never occurred since nations first came into existence. But at that time your people shall be delivered, everyone who is found written in the book. Many of those who sleep in the dust of the earth shall awake, some to everlasting life, and some to shame and everlasting contempt. Those who are wise shall shine like the brightness of the sky, and those who lead many to righteousness, like the stars forever and ever.
>
> Daniel 12:1–3

The great protector, the angel Michael, will see that justice is done not just for those who are living, but also for the dead. While the Hebrew Bible does not concern itself with many life-after-death stories, here the promise of life for those who are "wise" gives hope that even in death justice will come. (See also Zech. 38:8.)

Experiencing Holism

This "day," however, is not just about the absence of oppression, sickness, and other afflictions. Rather it is about a whole community living its life to the full as God intends. The imagery of this future hope throughout the prophets is often breathtaking. Here are some of the characteristics of what peaceful life will be like after "The day of the Lord."

Joyful

Isaiah 35:10 says that "the ransomed of the LORD shall return, and come to Zion with singing; everlasting joy shall be upon their heads; they shall obtain joy and gladness, and sorrow and sighing shall flee away." This inner joy stands in stark contrast to being the "ransomed" ones in exile. Rather than being oppressed—inside and out—God's people will be free to return to their city having "everlasting joy," which defeats the heavy "sighs" and "sorrow" their capture brought. (See also Isa. 9; Mal. 4:2; Jer. 30:9.)

Justice

The day when justice is normal and not exceptional is found throughout the prophets. For example, Isaiah points back to the best of the judges as a taste of what the day and the new community will be like.

> And I will restore your judges as at the first, and your counselors as at the beginning. Afterward you shall be called the city of righteousness, the faithful city. Zion shall be redeemed by justice, and those in her who repent, by righteousness. But rebels and sinners shall be destroyed together, and those who forsake the LORD shall be consumed.
>
> Isa. 1:26–28

Righteousness and justice are again paired as an expression of the social and institutional fairness that is envisioned and longed for. Those who had thwarted this have been taken away. (See also Isa. 11:4; 24:21–23; 29:20–21; Dan. 12:14; Joel 2:2–11.)

Salvation

Salvation in the Hebrew Bible speaks primarily of "well-being." It was not necessarily about the saving of souls or life after death, as many think of salvation today. The prophets associated salvation with the Lord being recognized for who he is, and therefore all being well in the world. As Isaiah prophesies: "The LORD is exalted, he dwells on high; he filled Zion with justice and righteousness; he will be the stability of your times, abundance of salvation, wisdom, and knowledge; the fear of the LORD is Zion's treasure" (Isa. 33:5–6).

Here justice, security, and worship are all bound together to describe what the new community of Zion will be like. (See also Isa. 9:2; 19:20–25; Dan. 12:10; Joel 2:32; Zeph. 3:17.)

Reconciliation between people

The lead-up to the day of the Lord will also usher in a new day in relationships between people. Restitution will come, and healthy relationships will result. In the very last words of the Hebrew Bible, Malachi writes, "Lo, I will send you the prophet Elijah before the great and terrible day of the LORD comes. He will turn the hearts of parents to their children and the hearts of children to their parents, so that I will not come and strike the land with a curse" (Mal. 4:5–6).

One of the first relationships to buckle under the pressure of oppression is family relationships. When this new peace comes, ushered in by a new Elijah, these relationships will be among the first to be healed. There is also the promise of reconciliation between tribes (Isa. 11:13) and nations (Isa. 19:23–24).

Reconciliation of nature

One of Malachi's comments concerns the land. The returning, redemption, and healing of land are all a part of the history of

103

redemption. We would be foolish to be so human-centered that we do not consider the role of the well-being of the environment and nature in God's plans. A typical image of this is found in Joel 2:21–22: "Do not fear, O soil; be glad and rejoice, for the LORD has done great things! Do not fear, you animals of the field, for the pastures of the wilderness are green; the tree bears its fruit, the fig tree and vine give their full yield."

Here the prophet is addressing nature directly. He tells the soil, animals, and plants that they matter to the Lord, and that he is concerned for their well-being. The promise is that the Lord will ensure that the balance of the natural order will be returned. The reconciliation between God and humans, God and nature, and humans and nature is a triangular relationship that will be at peace on that day. (See also Isa. 11:6–7; 35:9; 40:4; Joel 2:22.)

The coming of a just, compassionate, and anointed leader

The hope of the day of the Lord's arrival begins by concentrating on the arrival of a special leader, one who can make *shalom* happen. For example,

> For a child has been born for us, a son given to us; authority rests upon his shoulders; and he is named Wonderful Counselor, Mighty God, Everlasting Father, Prince of Peace. His authority shall grow continually, and there shall be endless peace for the throne of David and his kingdom. He will establish and uphold it with justice and with righteousness from this time onward and forevermore. The zeal of the LORD of hosts will do this.
>
> Isa. 9:6–7

As Christians, we believe this Messiah came in Jesus, the one who has the authority to usher in the vision of *shalom* and justice and the universal recognition of Yahweh. (See also Isa. 19:19; 28:16; 40:5; 43:4; 44:12–13, 26; 60:19–20; Jer. 23:5–6; Ezek. 34:2; Joel 2:23; Micah 4:1–2; Zech. 14:9–16.)

What do the prophets have to say about poverty? Perhaps it is simply that there is an alternative vision to the survival-of-the-fittest mentality that drives so many people, groups, and systems. There is a need to name the realities of oppression and injustice, to warn of the dire consequences they bring to those oppressing, and the harm they cause the poor. The prophets encourage us to work hard toward a different vision—a vision of hope, joy, and peace that is only possible by trusting Yahweh above every other authority. This change is required today if the world is not to destroy itself with its own greed and selfishness.

Of course, the prophets kept pointing back to the creator God as the one who would make this possible. As we will see in the next chapter, how God ushered in his new reign was a surprise to all.

Personal Reflection: It Only Takes a Spark

It was gone. I did know this. I had seen it on the TV news and in the newspapers, but as I peered through a gap in the corrugated-iron fence barrier, it was only then that it registered with me. The Suan Plu squatter settlement was no more. Where a thriving community of over 7,000 people had once lived, there was now just a rough, flattened, black dust heap. A fire had wiped it out in a matter of hours. A few people were picking through the debris, and some concrete structures jutted out of the dark ash, but even these remnants would soon be gone.

Good friends of ours, Dave and Kerry Verkade, had lived in Suan Plu for over eight years. While on sabbatical in 1999, I had helped to teach English to kids there with them. The Verkades had initiated an amazing microenterprise employing over thirty women. They had taught English and shared their lives and faith with neighbors in what was a congested, dark, rabbit warren of a neighborhood. If anybody was seeking the *shalom* of their city, it was Dave and Kerry. At the time of the fire (April 2004) the Verkades were out of Suan Plu with family from New Zealand for Kerry's birthday and were not physically harmed. However, their small home, their possessions, and their microenterprise project was gone.

How do you respond to such devastation?

Dave and Kerry went to be with their friends at the makeshift tent neighborhood on a local football ground. They started the microenterprise with the women again and have been supporting as best they can the plans for rebuilding Suan Plu. They quickly set up their home in a local shopfront with some of their neighbors. This seeking of *shalom* in solidarity has meant their life has been put on hold. As I write this, after twenty months of waiting, rebuilding has begun.

Other Christians, however, did not stand in solidarity with Suan Plu like Dave and Kerry did. They did not work holistically. Only a few weeks after the fire, a prayer e-mail was passed on to me. It said that revival had taken place in Suan Plu because of the fire. Hundreds of Buddhists had been converted to Christ. I inquired about this with Dave and Kerry. What had actually happened was that some Christians had announced over a loudspeaker that they had food parcels to give out. A crowd turned up and then, in addition to giving the parcels, they asked people to become Christians. Most felt desperate and obligated, and some consented to save the face of the Christians and themselves. Dave said, "People were thankful for any help they could get, but the Christian response annoyed them. They were asking, 'If this God loves us so much, where was he when our houses were burning down?'"

Anji calls these kinds of revival stories "Christian urban myths." Christians proclaim and perpetuate false myths about the nature of life and mission. It feels like Christian mission has become a series of Jenny Craig dieting stories where the before and after shots are taken. These stories are often unverifiable. Upon closer inspection, few of them live up to their claims. A Christian public, however, has got the story they like to hear, and pass it on like a whisper that becomes bigger and better with every telling. What is expected as "normal" in mission and ministry is now distorted. I'm sure the question came, "Dave and Kerry, why didn't you see the revival happen like this group?"

We live in an age of instant e-mails that can give the impression of success, but there are a few Nathans asking about our use of this power. We need those who are concerned for our long-term well-being, sensitive to God's promptings, and secure enough in a relationship to tell us the truth sometimes.

I know only a few people like this for me, but I value those few as highly as any relationship I have in life. I don't expect these people—the likes of Daryl Gardiner, Mark Watt, Mick Duncan, John Gilmore, and all the UNOH members—to always get it right with me. Yet, the risk of trust together far outweighs the isolation, alienation, and loss of perspective if I don't. A person who has been this kind of prophet for me and the UNOH community has been Mick Duncan. In a variation on this theme, he and Ruby Duncan introduced to our community the differences in leadership styles between "chief" and "medicine man or woman" in traditional tribal societies. The actual idea came from their fellow Kiwis, Renier Greeff and Trevor W. King, in their book *Medicine Man Chief*, but it seemed to have added authority when it was being presented by Mick and Ruby. They explained that, in this theory, the "chief's" main role is to seek the long-term well-being of the tribe (read: organization, school, church, nation). Perhaps this idea of "chief" is similar to what Jim Collins terms a "level 5" leader in his book *Good to Great*. Collins compared a range of similar companies and found that those that had "larger-than-life, celebrity leaders who ride in from outside are negatively correlated with taking a company from good to great." The charismatic, dynamic CEOs were not helpful over the longer term, but those who were "modest and willful, humble and fearless" were. Collins notes that a key role with this kind of leadership is not only to get the right people on the bus (read: company) and sit in the right places (read: play the right role), but also to protect the company by getting the wrong people out of the wrong seats or off the bus altogether. The "chiefs" then work out where the tribe could go to be healthy and effective with the right people. In so many ways this was what good kings did for the Hebrew people and what good chiefs do in healthy tribal societies.

What I find most interesting in this discussion is the leadership a medicine man or woman performs. This kind of leadership is not so straightforward, up front, or even viewed as leadership by some. The medicine man lives on the edge, away from the center. The medicine man's role is only there when the chief and others from the tribe ask for the medicine. If the medicine works, then by word of mouth more will come to recognize the medicine man or woman and seek out their help. A good medicine man or woman is the holder of mysteries, wisdom, and insights for the tribe. Whereas the "chief" is most concerned about the long-term well-being of the tribe, the medicine man or woman is loyal primarily to the truth. In many ways the good Hebrew prophets were the ones who offered truth as good medicine for the Hebrew people.

Mick first challenged me about this and my role in UNOH. I then asked him and Ruby to address the whole UNOH community about it. Was I more like the medicine man or the chief? Was my medicine only to be called upon when required, or was my role more to protect and nurture UNOH's future? In many ways I had behaved like a medicine man, but then at other times I acted like a chief. To complicate things further, the members of the UNOH community were like medicine men or women to the broader church, calling for more radical faithfulness. Yet, we had to come back to the question of what my role was inside the UNOH community. No wonder we were having trouble with my role! After a long discussion together, facilitated by Mick and Ruby, we all believed my role at that time in UNOH was as a chief. Not long after this discussion, the members and then board of reference of UNOH commissioned me as UNOH director for another five years. We were all clearer about what mandating this role meant. It took a medicine man like Mick Duncan to help us find the way forward, in a role that was similar to the best of the Hebrew prophets.

All of us need prophetic ministry. When Anji and I believed it was time for us to serve in the developing world, we had to trust those who were affected by the decision and include their voice. They had to surrender their dreams for us, and we had to surrender this dream of serving so that there could be the possibility of real discernment. We needed to be sure that a "no" could be heard before a decision could be reached. The first time this happened in 1997 there was a clear but disappointing "no"; Vietnam and the timing of us leaving Melbourne were not right for us. When we had this sense again in 2000, this time for Bangkok, we got a "yes"; the timing and place were right, and both sending and receiving communities agreed. I shudder to think what would have happened if we had just gone in 1997, without the checks and balances of a prophetic community around us. Most probably, there would be no UNOH community.

The role of prophetic ministry does not mean we don't test out what is said. We need to critique the critics. This is especially true in my role as a kind of chief in UNOH, as it is often my call about whether a course of action or a person playing a certain role will work towards UNOH's long-term well-being (or not). Of course, there are many well-meaning but false prophets out there. Some even have devious motivations, using others and seeking their own justifications and narrow agendas. Perhaps even more dangerous are those who are unaware of projecting their aspirations and mess onto others.

The challenge, then, is to journey with people who can be potential prophets for us over a period of time so that, when the crunch comes, we know whether their medicine is good or bad. We need to know that they are offering truth and that our long-term well-being as a community will have every chance of being enhanced.

What can we do so that we have more solidarity and less exploitation in Christ's name? How can we see more holistic responses to communities and not the propagation of falsities? The quiet, personal, authentic serving required in difficult places of discipleship will never have the success appeal of Christian urban myths. The kind of leadership required to help Christian workers do this over the long term is not appealing, even to the few activists who want to do this kind of ministry. Yet, if by the grace of God we can raise up and support a few more prophets who are able to stand with the poor and those serving the poor, I think we will have a fighting chance. Mandating leaders with clear personal and structural accountability is a crucial way forward for most Christian groups. It happened with David and Nathan—and it can happen again with us, too.

Consider the frightening alternative if we don't make these efforts. The lies, abuses of power, and oppression by those who want to help the poor become almost inevitable. Without defining the kinds of space and roles required, a madness can set in, an insanity that beset many of the Hebrew prophets and kings who missed the voice of God from the margins. We need both the kings and the prophets to "seek the *shalom* of the city" together. Perhaps this partnership could give us a fighting chance to help the unfashionable term "radical" to be redeemed. Isn't the radical change the prophets outlined what most Christians should hope for? Real and lasting transformation, including the end of poverty as we know it, could come if we take their critiques, warnings, and hope personally.

Questions for Discussion

- What is the nature of the power that prophets and kings have according to the Bible verses outlined in this chapter? How could this power be used or abused in relation to the poor?
- On a scale from 1 to 10, where David is a "1" and Nathan is a "10," what number would you give yourself regarding your own courage in situations of injustice? Why?
- What lack of freedoms outlined by the prophets do you see as most urgent to address today? Why?
- If you could imagine your community experiencing *shalom*, how would it be different from today?

A Personal Exercise

Find a quiet place to be with the Lord. For five minutes, try to still your mind and just sense God's loving gaze on you. Then, visualize the Lord sending you a Nathan. Try and picture Nathan's eyes and face. Nathan has come to you to challenge you about your biggest abuse of power towards the poor.

Allow him to speak, and write down everything he would say to you. Don't try to critique his voice or the exercise until after he has finished speaking.

Reflect

- What was true for you in this challenge? What was not?
- What do you think God is calling you to do from this? What would it take to go and do it?
- Share this with your community, and seek advice before doing what needs to be done to seek restitution.

The Gospels and Messianic Transformations

Opening Reflection: Abe Young's Offer

Abe puffed out his cheeks and patted his horse's neck. "Not long to go now, old boy." The road was hot and dusty, and he could feel particles of dirt starting to congeal at the back of his throat. No amount of coughing seemed to displace them.

Turning to one of his associates, Abe asked, "Do we really need to go all the way out here to see this guy and his land? Can't we just take the guy's word for it that he'll get us the money?"

The associate smiled and tilted his head slightly, squinting at Abe. "Sir, you don't have to come. We have it under control. You don't have to see it all for yourself. Your father used to love coming with us, though. Made a killing out of acquiring land from peasants like these. If they don't pay back the loans, we get their land. You know these jobs have given your family household everything you need and more. He'd make it an enjoyable day out for us all, too—gave us extra wine on the way home, your old man did, but you . . . maybe you might be more comfortable back with your scholar friends."

Abe wriggled in his saddle and looked down at the back of his horse's neck, clenching the reins tight in one hand and twisting its thick brown mane with the other.

"Well . . . guess it's what I have to do now that I'm in charge . . . see how it all works. If people don't pay back our loans, where would we all be? Just . . . just let's get this over with . . . quickly."

By early evening Abe and his associates made it to the peasant's property. Even in the fading light it looked more like an abandoned paddock than a vineyard, with dried-out vines hanging over old wooden fences.

"We gave a loan to these guys?" Abe asked.

"Yeah, a big one. Used to make great wine here, and your dad loved to drink here, too, but when the drought lasted over a year, it just wiped out all the farms around. Must have done something wrong to deserve this curse, I reckon, but you, my blessed friend, have all the extra wealth to keep this land until the drought breaks. Then you can have some laborers grow juicy red grapes again . . ."

Abe's mind flashed backed to thoughts of his dad, wine goblet in hand, toasting his latest acquisitions and his faithful workers. His stomach tightened at the thought of his father's recent death. How would he be able to support a household of over 300 family members and workers? "I won't let you down, Dad," he murmured to himself.

"Here he comes now," said the associate. "Brought the wife and kids with him, too, for a bit a sympathy, I expect." The family wore dirty shirts that used to be white or cream, and seeing the entourage, they rushed toward them. Kneeling down in the dust, they pleaded in unison, "Please, please don't take our land, it's been in our family for generations . . . We'll pay you back, we will . . ." Abe looked down, but the sight of the toddlers' pencil-thin legs and arms through their stained shirts, yellow-tipped hair, and bloated stomachs was too much; he could only look away, trying not to embarrass himself further by throwing up. The associate jumped off his horse and moved in. "Look, pal, you got your loan, you didn't pay, and now we have to sort out the difference. No one forced you to get a loan; you must be a sinner of some sort to be cursed this badly . . . We don't want to force you off our land . . . But we have families, too, you know . . . What can we do?"

As the associate grabbed the peasant father by the shoulder, a torrent of wailing came from the rest of the family. Abe kicked his horse and rode away from the distraught family. "I need to go pray," said Abe to himself as much as to his associates, who grinned at the young man's obvious discomfort. "Didn't think you were up to it to see how your wealth's made. We'll sort it out, boss, like we always do. Don't worry."

Under a tree a few hundred yards away, Abe was out of breath. He lifted up his cloth tunic, which was wet through with perspiration, and tried to fan it dry. With his eyes wide open, he cried out to the skies, "Lord, what do I need to have a real life, one pleasing to you, one that supports my household?" He turned away from the farmyard and wiped his face, making sure the associates wouldn't see his tears dripping down. He needn't have worried, as they had their hands full in the dusty scuffle. Just then Abe looked up to the heavens again. He felt a sense of peace come over him. He couldn't quite explain it, but it was as if he would be given an answer soon, a way out of this mess.

The entourage stayed the night at the farmhouse, but Abe didn't sleep much. He couldn't get rid of the howls of the skinny kids, and wondered if they would come back to get their revenge. Yet there was still this strange peace, as if he would soon receive an answer, and he eventually drifted off to sleep.

Just after dawn he was awakened by a commotion outside the farmhouse. "It's him, it's really him." A crowd of villagers were running down the road, kicking up dust as they did.

"Who is that?" Abe asked his associate, getting off his bed.

"Ah, don't worry. It's just that rabbi from Nazareth . . . You know, thinks he's the Messiah or something. The peasants just love him, though."

"This I have to see," Abe said, trying to keep cool.

"I bet he would be eager to see you, too, boss. Doesn't look like he's got a good benefactor, judging by the rabble that's around him, that's for sure."

If there was one thing Abe did know, it was how to charm influential people. He had been doing it all his life. The knack of becoming buddies with the rich and powerful had actually been an important part of his family's wealth and prestige. As he followed the crowd, Abe reminded himself of his gifts. *Act humble, flatter, ask a few leading questions to get him talking, and the rabbi will be won over in no time, too. Perhaps he could help me out of my predicament, or work out what else I need to do.*

The smell of peasant body odor, dust, and farm animals was getting to Abe, and he was out of breath again as the crowd parted so he could see the rabbi. Time for the charm.

"Good teacher, what must I do to inherit eternal life?"

A bit forward, but hey, I'm putting it all out there for him.

"Why do you ask me about what is good? There is only one who is good. If you wish to enter into life, keep the commandments," the young rabbi answered.

Ooh. Not quite so glad to see me after all. Need another question to get him going . . .

"Which ones?"

That should do it. Teachers just love to teach and work out priorities and stuff. I'll win him over whether he likes it or not.

"You shall not murder, you shall not commit adultery, you shall not steal, you shall not bear false witness, honor your father and mother, and also you shall love your neighbor as yourself."

That's all—kindergarten stuff. No divine answers here. Surely there is more to it than this. Oh no, he is turning to others, I'm losing him.

"I have kept all these—what do I still lack?"

Surely I need more than that old stuff? Although yesterday was quite traumatic. Doesn't he know I'm not like the other peasants, who don't even know how to greet a rabbi properly?

Ah, but my comment did bring a smile to his face. Wow, now things are getting warmer. That look in his eye is almost bringing a tear to my eyes. It's like he's looking deep within me . . .

"If you wish to be perfect, go, sell your possessions, and give the money to the poor, and you will have treasure in heaven; then come, follow me."

Abe fell to the ground. There was too much at stake to follow this line anymore. *I'm not one of these smelly fishermen. I have lots of people depending on me.*

But the rabbi and the crowd stood waiting, still looking at the young man, waiting for his response to Jesus's offer. What would his answer be? Abe could just swallow, turn from the crowd and the rabbi, and walk back to the farm and his waiting associates. There was a deep pain in his stomach. *Surely there is another answer as to how to inherit eternal life?*

✝

Of course, the above is a dramatization of the story of the rich young ruler found in Matthew 19:16–30, Mark 10:17–31, and Luke 18:18–30. We don't actually know the man's name or much of his background, but I have tried to help us imagine what it could have been like for him so we can better engage with what Jesus has to say about poverty. Jesus's response to him was not like the welcome pack, free coffee, and cake that most rich people encounter when they have questions of faith for today's ministers.

(Prayerfully read Matthew's version in 19:16–30 as if you were the rich young ruler.)

Many Christians are more like the rich young ruler than any other New Testament character. Well-resourced, bright, charming, able to engage in religious discussion—talk about poverty, even—but unable to even comprehend what Jesus invites them to do and be. Seriously, what if Jesus said to you, "Go, sell your possessions and give the money to the poor, and you will have treasure in heaven; then come, follow me" (Matt. 19:21)?

What voices inside us would rise up to squash a response before we could even consider it and demand that we cling to what we already have? Too many are leaving Jesus "sad," for all they have is "much wealth."

The Bible's Call: Discipleship, God's Reign, and Ending Poverty

Let's look more closely at this invitation to discipleship and its meaning for us today in ending poverty. In Matthew's version of this small story, I see some of the most important themes relating to how oppression can be ended.

"Go"

The rich young ruler rightly recognizes that Jesus is a teacher with authority. His formal approach, flattery, and questions all indicate he knew something of Jesus's importance and how to treat a highly regarded rabbi. Yet, whenever someone in Matthew's Gospel uses the title "teacher" for Jesus, they always leave Jesus disappointed. For example, a scribe says to Jesus, "Teacher, I will follow you wherever you go" (Matt. 8:19). After Jesus explains that this following will mean having "nowhere to lay his head," we hear no more of the scribe. The Pharisees (Matt. 9:11), scribes and Pharisees (Matt. 12:38), collectors of temple taxes (Matt. 17.24), Pharisees and Herodians (Matt. 22:16), Sadducees (Matt. 22:24), and a lawyer (Matt. 22:36) all are outfoxed by Jesus when they use rhetoric to try to trap him to suit their own ends. What they all have in common is questionable motives. None are sincere in wanting to learn from the one they address as "teacher." Given that the rich young ruler is quick to call Jesus "teacher," we have a clue that he, too, misses Jesus's significance and call to transformation.

This clue is confirmed when Jesus says, "Go," and the rich man does not. "Go" is a non-negotiable command. In Matthew we find that it is always linked with authority. This is explained by the centurion—a Gentile oppressor, no less—who tells Jesus that he doesn't have to come to his house to heal his daughter because "I also am a man under authority, with soldiers under me; and I say to one, 'Go,' and he goes, and to another, 'Come,' and he comes, and to my slave, 'Do this,' and the slave does it." Jesus is amazed at such faith, and sees it as a taste of what is to come, when "outsiders" become "insiders." Jesus then turns to the centurion and commands him, "Go; let it be done for you according to your faith." Jesus's authority is such that when Jesus says, "Go," the centurion's daughter is healed "in that hour" (Matt. 8:5–13).

Matthew has further examples of this demonstration of Jesus's authority. Lepers are told to "go" as a part of their healing (Matt. 8:4); demons are told to "go" as a part of exorcism (Matt. 8:31); a paralytic is told to "go" as part of his healing; and mourners are told to "go" because a girl is not dead, but only asleep (Matt. 9:24).

"Go" is also used by Jesus to command disciples to act. They are to "go" over to the other side of the lake, and to "go" first only to the lost sheep of the house of Israel (Matt. 10:6). Then, of course, after the resurrection they are told that "all authority" has been given to Jesus, and he therefore tells them to "go and make" disciples of all nations (Matt. 28:18–20).

There is never any ambiguity in these calls to obedience. The only options are to obey or disobey, with all the consequences that this might have. The question to "go" (or not) is raised in Jesus's parable about two sons (Matt. 21:28–32). A father asks both sons to "go and work in the vineyard today." The first says he will not go, but does. The other says he will go, but doesn't. Jesus then asks those in the temple listening to him, "Which of the two did the will of his father?" They say, "The first." Jesus says to them, "Truly I tell you, the tax collectors and the prostitutes are going into the kingdom of God ahead of you." To disobey the word "go" was to stand against a direct authority. Going is, then, linked with authority and obedience, something Jesus said that the most unlikely people would understand and respond to.

By using "go" Jesus underlines his own authority. The question of control and authority would have been important for the rich young ruler. "What good deed must I do to have eternal life?" was his question. He wanted something from Jesus to be able to inherit this life as he had inherited his wealth, but he would not obey Jesus. This is not true faith. Anthropologist Bronislaw Malinowski claims that there is a difference between magic and true religion. Magic attempts to manipulate spiritual forces so that the supplicants can get what they want. But true religion is about surrendering to God so that God can do, through the supplicant, what God wants. The rich young ruler would not surrender all to Jesus, and his lack of obedience is evidence that he was more interested in magic than true faith.

The struggle of faith over magic is as crucial today as it was in previous ages. I witness obvious attempts at magic most days here in Klong Toey. Some magic transactions are simple, such as the use of spirit houses. In most neighborhoods here, these little dollhouse-like structures are set on poles, and are complete with miniature furniture and people inside. Neighbors give fresh fruit and burn incense as a way of appeasing the local spirit, and for good luck. While I obviously don't agree with this, I can see the way it works in my neighbors' minds.

I don't understand some of the other attempts at magic here, though. Down at the local market, for example, most nights you can see middle-aged men wandering around with magic belts. Various-sized phallic wooden carvings hang from these belts. I am told they are intended to help fertility—an ancient, magical form of Viagra. What I don't understand is why they would advertise!

Sometimes it is easier to see magic in cultures other than our own. Perhaps in the context of a globalized, consumer-driven culture, we have become more vulnerable to magic than we care to admit. Certainly, the magical instinct is exploited by most advertising campaigns. If you drive this car or wear this perfume or have this house, your life will be fulfilled. If we name these sorts of assumptions as magic, there is a lot at stake, because our whole economic system is built around us getting what we want. This includes the use of magic by the church. Too much contemporary Christianity is more like magic than true faith. A wander down the aisles of most Christian bookstores will yield numerous books on attempts to manipulate spirit forces with the right formulas, too. These books are not about surrendering all to Jesus so that

God can do through us what God wants. They are attempts to help consumers get what they want.

Such magic, however, doesn't fulfill us, and we keep searching for more to consume. "If I only had the right book or program or insight or church, then God would give me what I want." This is a long way from Jesus's command to "deny yourself, take up your cross, and follow me."

Like the rich young ruler, we can't do deals with Jesus. The ruler wanted to magically inherit eternal life, but was not willing to surrender his life to Jesus and his desire for the poor. As we will see, those who become Jesus's disciples can't do deals beforehand. They must surrender to Jesus first and then let him do through them whatever he wants to do.

The rich young ruler did not dispute the authority of Jesus or the rightness of Jesus's invitation, but he did not go. If we are to be Jesus's disciples, we must recognize Jesus's authority, this word "go," and obey this commission, especially those of us who have inherited wealth.

"Sell your possessions and give the money to the poor, and you will have treasure in heaven"

Jesus then makes plain what form this surrender to his authority will take. The rich young ruler needed liberation from his possessions, but, as we will soon see, it was those same possessions that possessed him. The nature of households in first-century Palestine would have been similar to those hinted at in the opening reflection. Being considered "wealthy" or "rich" in Jesus's day would have meant being responsible for the livelihoods of hundreds of people. So Jesus did not say "sell all you have" lightly. Jesus knew the implications for him and those for whom he was responsible.

Why, then, would Jesus insist on him selling everything?

Perhaps Jesus's summary of the law gives us a clue, which I tried to flesh out in my dramatization. In all the Gospels, Jesus quotes the six ethical teachings of the "ten commandments" (the first four "theological" ones were left out). Interestingly, however, in Matthew the last commandment ("do not covet what belongs to your neighbors") is replaced with "you shall love your neighbor as yourself." In Mark it is replaced with "do not defraud." What both are saying to us is that Jesus was concerned about how the man became rich.

How would those of us from Australia answer Jesus? The answers would not be pretty. As a part of the British colonization of Australia, land was taken and its custodians oppressed, persecuted, and killed. This "empty land" was then transplanted with British thinking, technologies, and, of course, unwanted prisoners.

It is a strange thing for me to now live in Asia and be asked, "How did Australia get so white?"

It is actually a horrifying story, which includes disobedience to all of the things Jesus cites to the rich young ruler as basic to our faith—do not kill, do not rape, do not lie, honor parents, love neighbors as self. However, like the rich young ruler, few Australians today would own up to breaking these commands. "All these I have kept since I was young," we would say.

To test this out, I sent out an e-mail to a few "wild" preachers I know who have preached on this story and wouldn't pull any punches. What I asked for were real excuses that they had heard for not observing this commandment. Below is what I got back, in order of the most feral.

Top ten reasons this invitation to discipleship doesn't apply to me:

- "Yeah, but if we all did that, who would support the missionaries?"
- "Yeah, but God has called me to minister to the rich. You have to be like them to be respected by them."
- "Yeah, it's on my to-do list. Just after I finish university/get this promotion/get the house renovated/after the kids leave school/when I retire."
- "Jesus only asked that of him because he had problems with possessions (but I don't)."

121

- "Jesus only asked that of him because he didn't have a family (but I do)."
- "Actually, you really can take your possessions through the 'eye-gate' in the Jerusalem wall so long as the camel bows its knees to get through." (There never was such a gate until the middle ages, when the church made it up . . . but it lives on!)
- "No, Jesus wants us all to have the best. Even his garment was so fantastic that the Roman guards gambled for it."
- "Of course, I would give it all up tomorrow . . . if Jesus made it clear to me that's what he wanted."
- "I already give my ten percent. What's this? The bigger commission?"
- "Giving money to the poor just isn't good stewardship—they just waste it on booze 'n' stuff."

The point of Jesus's command is not to make us wallow in guilt about possessions, but to force us to acknowledge our sin and seek restitution. That is why Jesus points out the need to "sell all you have and give it to the poor." We need to find personal responses to benefiting from unjust structures. There are limited resources on the earth. There is enough for all to live well. All should have enough food, clothes, and medicine, but there is not enough for all of us to live well-off. If everyone on the planet drove a car, there would be no oil. One person's excess is another's shortfall.

This is why Jesus didn't ask for the money himself. He wanted the rich young ruler to make poverty and injustice personal. He couldn't give it to a charity. He actually had to meet the poor himself. The ones he had not loved as himself, he had to go and visit personally.

Who were these people? Who are the poor? The Greek word for poor here (*ptochoi*) isn't very helpful; the Greeks only had one word for "poor," and it was used in various ways. When we read through the whole Bible, we find numerous names for the poor. As we have seen, the basic theme is about people and groups who are oppressed, marginalized, or lacking power. In the Hebrew Bible, there are five different names for those facing poverty. Each gives a subtle variation on the identity of those facing poverty, with whom we all must engage if we are to obey Jesus:

- *chacer*—those who lack or are inadequate in some way. For example, the *chacer* lack "food" (Job 30:3; Deut. 28:57; Amos 4:6), shelter (Prov. 6:32), or wisdom. This word is used thirty-six times.
- *ruwsh*—those who are dispossessed. For example, the *ruwsh* have been dispossessed of land, possessions, and dignity (2 Sam. 12:1–4; Prov. 18:23; 22:7). This word is used thirty-one times.
- *dal*—those who are frail, weak, and helpless. For example, the oppressed *dal* need help from those with the power to provide help (Exod. 23:3; Lev. 14:21; 1 Sam. 2:8; Job 20:19; Isa. 26:6; Amos 8:6). This word is used fifty-seven times, most often translated into English as "the poor."
- *ebyown*—those who are in need and dependent. The *ebyown* have no resources of their own and so depend on the charity and justice of others (Amos 4:1; Isa. 14:30; 25:4). This word is used sixty-one times, most often translated as "the needy" and often used with *dal*.
- *aniy*—those who are oppressed. The *aniy* are exploited and crushed by the powerful (2 Sam. 22:28; Job 36:15; Ps. 9:18; 12:5; 14:6; Isa. 14:32; 26:6). This word is used the most of the five words in the Hebrew Bible; it is used eighty times.

These words describe the marginalization and oppression that the poor face and experience to the core of their very identity. The poor tend to internalize their marginalization and oppression. This affects their view of themselves and their place in the world; it makes them feel less than human.

Oscar Lewis, an anthropologist, did research into what he would call the "culture of poverty" that emerged from within migrant groups that were marginalized from the mainstream or oppressed in any way. Some of the characteristics that emerged include:

- suspicion and apathy toward the institutions within society;
- the production of little wealth and receiving little back in return;
- unemployment and the resulting lack of reserves of cash and food;
- acceptance of middle-class values, but failure to live by them;
- hostility toward and mistrust of government and police;
- uncherished or unprotected childhood;
- a strong emphasis on the present and immediate gratification;
- preoccupation among men to prove their masculinity.

It is so easy for those not from a culture of poverty to be judgmental—of drug users, for example—and say they don't deserve our help. Why don't they just say "no" and make their choices like "us"? However, communities that are characterized by the above Hebrew words, and the resulting culture of poverty, are more vulnerable to violence and drug use than those free of such injustice and oppression. If life seems hopeless, living for the moment is all you have, and something to numb the pain is a relief.

This sort of poverty can't be turned around simply by giving money, or even changing laws or political structures. It takes people full of hope and faith in Jesus to turn this despair around, as well as every law, structure, and technological resource at our disposal. While I live in a slum, this definition opens me up to poverty in its many forms everywhere. For example, what was remarkable about the fire in the Suam Plu slum was not only the courage of the community to try to regroup after the fire, but also the fact that not one of the 3,000 residents were killed or seriously injured. If it had happened in most neighborhoods in Australia, who knows how many would have been forgotten, isolated, left alone, or found burned among the ashes. A biblical understanding of poverty includes destitution, but its broader definition is the lack of ability to live as God intends. Poverty comes from a society that says you are only worthwhile insofar as you benefit me.

The rich and poor were segregated in Jesus's time (as now), so they did not naturally meet up. Jesus told a story of a rich man who doesn't even see a beggar at his door (Luke 16:19–31). Like the rich young ruler, issues of eternity are at stake here. The very question of eternal life that the rich young ruler raised is being answered. If you sell all you have and give it to the poor, "you will have treasure in heaven." The eternal question of what in this life is meaningful was answered, but the rich man didn't want to know about it. If we are to hear Jesus's call to discipleship, every Christian must make poverty personal. That includes poverty in the West, and not just in the most extreme situations.

It is not only our money that is needed; actual people are needed, too. True, we don't need the colonial motivations of missionaries in the past, but we do need the same sacrifices. What I have found is that if we share our money, we are considered generous. However, if we personally go and share our lives among the poor, we are considered as colonizers by the left, as Communists by the right, and just plain crazy by the rest. Yet, I believe the redistribution of resources must include people. Real flesh-and-blood people who are known personally can help form partnerships with indigenous Christian movements from anywhere.

The body of Christ is disabled, almost mutilated. Some parts are fat and obese, dripping with more jewelry than they can hold. Other parts of Christ's body are down to the bare bones, diseased and hurting. Will we be open to give up all for the sake of Christ, serving personally among the poor? Can we heal the body of Christ around the world?

"Come, follow me"

If the rich young ruler could have obeyed Jesus's command to "go" and then "give all to the poor," he would have been in a place to follow Jesus. He would not have been left destitute. He would have joined a community that was living out true faith in Christ, helping to establish the kingdom of God on earth.

We must be clear here about joining Jesus's community. Jesus preached, delivered, healed, and gave the message of the kingdom. Jesus's central concern was not socializing people into his church, but proclaiming the reign of God and seeing its authority heal and restore the most vulnerable. "Repent, for the kingdom of heaven has come near" (Matt. 4:17). There are 114 references to "God's reign" in Matthew, Mark, and Luke alone, but "church" is only mentioned four times (all in Matthew, and three times in one chapter [18] relating to resolving conflict). If we are to join Jesus, we must be prepared "to strive first for the kingdom of God and its righteousness" above all other agendas. Proclaiming the reign of God was Jesus's purpose, a foundation for everything else, and it must be ours, too, if we are to be faithful to Christ. Unfortunately, the term "kingdom of God" has become so cliché and domesticated it has lost most of its radical meaning. What, then, is the nature of this reign, and what has it to do with responding to poverty?

As we have seen, the Hebrew understanding of poverty is much broader than destitution. It could have been tempting to look at all those verses about poverty and conclude that poverty is simply powerlessness. The Hebrew people were oppressed in all kinds of ways because they did not have power. It could follow then that the answer to poverty is to give the poor lots of power. Certainly, many contemporary development workers define poverty in such terms.

This theme of poverty-as-powerlessness is right, but only to a point. There is a difference between power and true authority. The latter consists of being true to who God has made us to be and true to what we are given to do in God's world. Those in poverty, then, do not have the "authority" to live the full, healthy, and meaningful lives God intends for them. Simply gaining power, status, or wealth, then, are shallow answers to the deep problems faced by the poor. In post-colonial times in countries such as Cambodia, Vietnam, and Burma, simply gaining power (over and above others) just replaced one set of oppressors with another. What Jesus proclaimed and offered was authority to live as God intends.

As Christians, we believe Jesus is this hope of *shalom* realized—the ultimate revelation of what God intends. He is the Lord of *shalom* (2 Thess. 3:16) and is anointed to bring "good news to the poor" (Luke 4:18–19), fulfilling all the laws, including the jubilee laws. Jesus is the "anchor of the soul" and the hope of our faith (Heb. 6:19). Jesus could do this for us because he did not give in to temptation, even under persecution, torture, and execution. Therefore, only Jesus had the authority to choose real life and (sacrificial) death, and could offer this life, through his resurrection and the Spirit, to others. The disciples received this grace freely and could then go and offer Jesus's authority and life to others (Matt. 28:16–18). "Jesus is Lord" became an early faith statement proclaiming the reality that Jesus's authority was above all others, and that our own authority and freedom to live as God intends was linked intrinsically with this authentic authority and freedom.

The reign of God, then, is about the Lordship of Christ, or the *shalom* of God breaking through. Jesus's authority was shown whenever Jesus was in the midst of the people, when demons were cast out, and when healing and miracles in nature occurred. Jesus's teachings about this reign were often parables set in homes, marketplaces, or on the land, requiring us to risk all against anti-reigns in seeking first the reign of God and its justice. Jesus is the center and reference point of this reign of God; he turns upside-down the centers and reference points of those who only have power and not authority. This is what made Jesus's life so threatening. God could have entered our world as Jesus at any time, anywhere, so we must pay attention to how Jesus chose to live. If Jesus is the reference point of God's reign, then we need to conform to Jesus's life and image.

Jesus experienced poverty personally

Jesus was conceived out of wedlock. He fled persecution as a refugee to Egypt. He lived in an oppressed land as part of an oppressed people at the hands of the colonizing Romans. Jesus experienced hunger (Matt. 12) and homelessness (Matt. 8:20), and was discriminated against by both Romans and other Jews because he was from Nazareth. He was tortured, falsely tried, and murdered.

Jesus taught insights that offered authority to transform poverty "on earth as it is in heaven"

Jesus prayed for God's reign to come here on earth as in heaven (Matt. 6:10), and warned of a final day when the sheep and goats will be separated according to how they treated the "least of these." The goats included people like the rich man who missed the beggar, and the rich fool who stored up wealth. Jesus taught that the lure of wealth was like weeds that choke seeds. He cursed the rich and blessed the poor, but offered a kingdom community life where labels of rich and poor were not allowed. Jesus promised his presence to "be with" those who "go" and seek disciples of this coming kingdom.

Jesus used miracles to demonstrate the kingdom's coming

Jesus personally touched lepers and "unclean" women and made them whole again. He healed the blind on the Sabbath. He was able to multiply a few loaves and fish into enough to feed multitudes after his disciples gave what little they had to feed the hungry. He cast out oppressive evil spirits in people—often children, women, or those on the "other side" of society.

Jesus empowered Christian communities to live like him by dying, rising again, and giving his Spirit

Jesus showed that sacrifice until death is required to beat oppression. He showed by example how to live with others. He rose again from the dead as evidence of God's pleasure with this life. His Spirit was given so that all people, poor and non-poor alike, could continue his mission in the world and end poverty. Jesus's early church did this so well that they were all together and no one was in need (Acts 2:44–45).

How people respond or don't respond to "the least of these" (sick, homeless, hungry, jailed) is the litmus test of where we place our faith. Is our faith and trust in Jesus and the authority of his reign, or is it in the world's power? (Matt. 25:31ff.)

✠

The reign of God, then, is simply God's will being done on earth as it is in heaven. This is a liberating force like no other for those facing poverty. It turns upside-down the priorities of the authorities and powers of this world. The last are first and the first are last. Where people have lived unauthorized lives from the powers' point of view—able to be used and abused for the benefit of the elite—God has intervened by giving Jesus's life as the only true authority.

Jesus's life gave authority to the lives of the poor and gave a new reference point for all to see. This is not simply a narrow dogma or ideology to defend, but a living person. When people, groups, and systems start to live like Jesus, then all can have Jesus's authority to live out God's intended *shalom* together. This is the in-breaking reign of God that Jesus proclaimed. After the rich young ruler turned away, Jesus turned to the disciples. Those who are not poor often can't see the new kingdom coming because they have too much at stake in the old kingdom. While there was a promise to Peter that sacrificing all for Jesus now is nothing compared to what we get in kingdom terms, Peter was provoked to ask Jesus, "Who then can be saved?" A camel simply can't get through an eye of a needle. Jesus's answer to Peter was that "all things are possible for God." This invitation, then, is grace. No one is good enough to earn the kingdom. Jesus was turning upside-down the notion of the day that "blessing equals wealth." This was even more explicit in Jesus's sermon on the plain, where he said, "Blessed are you who are poor . . . but woe to you who are rich" (Luke 6:20, 24). The rich are not good enough, and the poor are not good enough; but the poor are generally under no illusions about their situation. Yet, Jesus promised that those who followed him would receive a bigger and better family. It doesn't take money to step out to receive and use the authority of Christ. The threats of persecution were named by Jesus here, too, not least because a powerful young ruler was now at odds with Jesus's community. By giving up everything and standing with the new family of Christ among the poor, however, the disciples would have more than enough family and places to stay, even if there were real threats.

The very real questions that faced the rich young ruler face us today. Will we give up everything to join the kingdom cause? Will we throw our lot in with a Christian community to live out our Christian discipleship? Will we be a part of the problem or part of the solution in ending oppression?

While the rich man said "no," Peter's life said "yes" to Jesus. For all his wealth and power, we don't even know the rich man's name. Yet, Peter is remembered and celebrated as one who experienced God's grace and authority, and who helped change the course of human history.

While researching and writing this chapter I stayed at my Klong Toey neighbor's family home at their fishing village in Prachuap, in south Thailand. Early one morning I walked along the beach when the fishing boats were coming in. The half dozen boats still had their green fluorescent lights on, each boat with two or three bleary-eyed men on board with catches in their nets, the small motors pushing the boats towards the shore. I couldn't help but think of Peter's invitation to discipleship and how different his response was from the rich young ruler's. He could have stayed with his family fishing business, but he "left everything" to follow Jesus. Sure, he didn't really have that much to lose compared with the rich young ruler. Yet, he was giving up something real and something that he knew. In the end, it was a small price to pay to help change the world and have an eternal impact.

Inviting Discipleship in an Unjust World

One of the common questions I get from people is, "Given the fact that there is so much poverty and misery all around you, do you get angry with God or doubt that God exists?" My only answer is that while I sometimes have moments where God is not foremost on my mind, I need Jesus here more than just about anywhere else I have been.

Let me give you an example. One morning one of our Burmese refugee neighbors was hanging around our front door. I invited him in, but I figured he really wanted to see Anji about his application to be repatriated to the U.S. But he kept hanging around the door a bit longer and eventually accepted my invitation to come in.

"Just had my health check," he said. His eyes were puffy, and he started to weep. "The doctor said I have AIDS. Could you ring him and see how long it will take before I die? I couldn't understand much. My wife hasn't come back from taking my son to school yet . . ." I don't know what you would do in that situation. The only thing I could think of was to ask Jesus to come and that his peace would comfort my friend, and plead for his healing.

I really had nothing else to offer in that moment except Jesus. In the end, when Anji came home, she organized for my friend to get a second opinion at our hospital. Later we found it wasn't full-blown AIDS. With the right medication, the doctor said he would more likely die from smoking than HIV. He promptly gave up smoking!

This got me thinking. There seems to be a crisis of confidence in evangelism today among many Christians. Sure, some will still take people to hear an American evangelist, but personally sharing our faith in Jesus with neighbors or friends, actually inviting them to become disciples of Jesus, seems to be at an all-time low.

We have to remember that Jesus's message isn't just talk. God's reign isn't just a good idea. It is about meeting a real person, Jesus, who can change the way things are to the way they should and can be. Sharing the good news should be about seeking how

God's will is being done on earth as it is in heaven. Jesus invited the poor and non-poor alike to participate in this cause. By grace, the authority to live as God intends is not far from any one of us. To live fully as children of God—this is the agenda that will have its final fulfillment in heaven but has already started.

Why would we want anybody to miss out on this good news, especially the ones who know that they face despair and oppression?

Personal Reflection: "Are We Blessed Yet?"—The Beatitudes and What Really Counts

The point of our faith is not to have bigger and better lives or churches, but to transform the world. Specifically, the body of Christ has the answer to poverty in both the developing and Western worlds. Yet, too often this answer is reduced to the cliché, "We are blessed to be a blessing." For Western Christians this "blessing" is often understood as material wealth. While some parts of the Hebrew Bible (for example, Deuteronomy 28) do seem to point to wealth as a sign of God's presence, the New Testament specifically undermines this notion of blessing. "Blessed are you who are poor . . . hungry . . . weeping . . . hated. Woe to you who are rich . . . well fed . . . laughing . . . spoken well of" (Luke 6:20–22). Real blessing is fulfilled in the person and presence of the risen Christ (Eph. 1:3). It is this Jesus who is anointed to liberate the poor (Luke 4:18–20) and who can inspire selfish human beings to become living sacrifices for others. "Blessed are those who are persecuted for righteousness' sake, for theirs is the kingdom of heaven" (Matt. 5:10). God's blessing today is not found in leather wallets, but among the cries of multitudes facing poverty. For there we find Jesus's presence longing to intervene through his body, the church.

The Western church does need to redistribute its wealth if it is to follow Jesus today. But, more than that, we need to make poverty personal by standing with Jesus among the poor and loving actual neighbors as ourselves. This will not come cheaply. There are enough resources in the world for us all to live well, but not well-off. For example, if everyone on the planet owned a car, there would not be enough fuel, and the pollution would cause a desert that only cockroaches and Mad Max could survive in. The last thing the Western church needs to do is to consume more resources. Yet, a recent Christian book proclaimed just that in its title: *You Need More Money!* This is despite the findings of David Barrett from the World Evangelization Research Center that "the church in World C [i.e., the Western church] spends 99 percent of its income on itself." Even if wealth did equal "blessing," the last group on earth in charge of redistributing it should be the Western church!

No! The body of Christ's answer to world poverty is more precious than mere silver or gold. Pastor Suwot, with whom we work here in Klong Toey, is an example of someone who experiences real blessing. Pastor Suwot was born and bred in Klong Toey, where his parents still live. He was a mafia boss, used and dealt in drugs, and spent time in jail. After locking himself in a room, he cried to Jesus for help and asked his parents to give him food under the door. He was detoxed in three days. Later Pastor Suwot went to a Bible school and then returned to Klong Toey. Church growth people say the natural momentum for people like Suwot is "redemption and lift." This is not a new kind of wonder bra, but a description of the social climbing that often happens once people get rid of obvious addictions and begin to fit in with a broader, wealthier network of Christian friends. Suwot resisted these impulses and returned to share his life and faith with those of his own background, something few poor people dare to do.

On Sunday mornings, our family—with some neighborhood kids in tow—walks from our home to the Ta Rua Church, founded by Pastor Suwot, at the other end of the slum. As we climb the stairs and enter through the doors of the third-story dwelling of a shopfront that also serves as Pastor Suwot's family home, many in the swaying congregation turn and give the traditional Thai greeting, the *wai*, to us. Wearing unassuming T-shirts and flip flops, many of the thirty members, some with physical disabilities, see each other most days. There is a tangible feeling that God's Spirit is at work here. This is the only Christian church for Klong Toey's 80,000 residents, which includes 79,900 or more Buddhists. Pastor Suwot greets us, talking in hushed tones at the back of the church about trying to start a soccer academy and gym to help keep despair at bay, and be a contact point for an increasingly desperate younger generation in the slum. Would we help?

Pastor Suwot sacrificially loves his neighbors as himself (the "royal law," according to James) and, therefore, this Christian community can offer a revolutionary blessing to the broader neighborhood—the presence of the crucified and risen Jesus. Jon Sobrino puts it this way: "What the Christian faith says is that God will grant definitive justice to the victims of poverty and, by extension, to those who have sided with them. This is an active hope, which unloosens creativity at all levels of human existence—intellectual, organizational, ecclesial—which is marked by notable generosity and boundless, even heroic, altruism" (*The Principle of Mercy*, 6).

The broader body of Christ can stand in solidarity creatively with Christian communities like this one in Klong Toey. This is exactly the kind of blessing the poor communities of the West and developing world need. They do not simply need more money! Our churches and lives are meaningful and distinctly Christian when they build our capacity to share this transformative blessing. Like the widow's mite or the Pharisee's gold, our generosity or stinginess will be judged by what we keep for ourselves and not simply what we seem to give.

Have we really been blessed to be a blessing yet? Pastor Suwot is more like Peter than the rich young ruler, but his eternal inheritance comes at a huge price emotionally and economically. It's a price Suwot and his family gladly share, but one which makes a difference on earth and in heaven. It's a blessing of incalculable worth.

Questions for Discussion

- In what ways are you like and unlike the rich young ruler?
- Why will the liberation of the poor be so important to God's reign?
- What makes a "Christian" response to poverty different from a "secular" response to poverty?
- What could God's blessing and restitution look like for you in following Jesus and his heart for the poor?
- In what ways have you experienced Jesus's authority to bring about change?

A Personal Exercise

- Put a piece of letter paper in a horizontal position.
- On the left-hand third, draw a picture/collage of what the world is like now in terms of poverty and oppression.
- On the right-hand third, draw a picture/collage of what the world would be like if God's reign fully came on earth as in heaven. Leave the middle third blank at this stage.
- Take some time to pray about both sides of the paper, asking:

  What most strikes you about this picture?

  What could be done to move the world from left to right?
- Draw some pictures or a collage in the middle, brainstorming possible solutions and addressing the barriers that cause poverty and oppression on the left-hand-side picture.
- Try something from your "middle third" that could help God's reign to come on earth as in heaven.

6

The Early Church
Standing Against Poverty Together

Opening Reflection: Peter's Return

Sure, Judas did the devil's dirty work, but I was worse. I ran as soon as they grabbed him. As if that wasn't enough, as I warmed myself by a fire, I even rejected Jesus when a little girl asked if I was with him. The cock crowed in the distance and I went into hiding among the shadows with the others. Everything went dark, including my life. We all fled for our lives, our hopes smashed on that execution device, along with our Lord. I'd given everything up for him, and then found that Jesus was not the leader I thought he was. Was there anything worth living for now?

Then a strange thing happened. Women came to us early the next morning and said that they saw two men, glowing, at Jesus's gravesite. They gave them the good news that Jesus was alive, and the women couldn't tell us fast enough! I didn't believe them, so

I ran to the tomb to see for myself. All I saw were some of the strips of his burial cloths. Jesus's body wasn't there, so I had no idea what really went on.

A few of us walked away from Jerusalem and the dream it represented, back to normal life as fishermen in Galilee, if we could manage it again. I was in a daze one morning, my arms tight and aching after a long night of fishing. Well, I say we went fishing, but we caught nothing.

A private confession: my family is not very good at fishing. In fact, we don't even have the right fishing gear. As we stood in the shallows mending those nets again, a smart aleck stranger asked, "Friends, do you have any fish?" Well, he could see our nets were empty, so we just said, "No." "Throw them on the other side, and you'll find some." We grinned and jokingly threw the net over the other side. We suddenly caught 153 fish, which was almost as much a miracle as the fact that our nets didn't break and need mending again!

I shouldn't have been surprised, but this stranger turned out to be Jesus. He made us breakfast, forgave me, and restored me again. With the others we began to have secret meetings back in Jerusalem with this one who was risen.

"It's about God's reign breaking through," the risen Jesus kept saying again and again during these times. We still didn't get it, even then. Someone asked, "Lord, are you at this time going to restore the kingdom to Israel?" We were sick of all the fear and oppression, having to sneak around all the time. If Jesus could defeat even death, wasn't it now time for our turn at executing power and justice? Surely we could defeat those invading Romans and anyone who sympathized with them.

Jesus looked at us with that deep love only he could give. His eyes almost seemed ablaze. He talked about giving us God's "authority" through the "Holy Spirit."

This would be an authority that would enable us to be witnesses and martyrs of this new reign all over the world. The promised Spirit was the sign of things to come all over the world, but it would start in Jerusalem. "Wait in Jerusalem for the Holy Spirit," was Jesus's last command to us during this time, before he went up into the sky.

A friend put us up in his house in the city. We had the upstairs part to ourselves and started praying, waiting for this new authority to arrive. Since our small apostolic community needed to be reordered, we took the time to replace Judas with Matthias and made sure the women, who had been so courageous all the way through, continued to have a special part in all this. That's when it happened. At first, it was like a hurricane ripping through us, almost knocking us to the floor. A flame of fire landed on each of us, but we weren't burned. Then, it was as though we were possessed and filled by this presence, and we began to overflow with languages we didn't understand. This got louder and louder until in pure ecstasy we were shouting as loud as our voices could hold.

Eventually, a crowd gathered around the bottom of our friend's house to see what was happening. It was a special holy day, so our people had come to Jerusalem from all over the world. The gibberish that overflowed in us was understandable to those who were there. The Holy Spirit spoke through us, using us as a channel for his wonders to be declared with authority. Most didn't get it, and some even started to make fun of us. "They're just drunks from Galilee."

Now, I wasn't prepared to hide or take anything like that anymore, so I stood up and, before I knew it, made the case that God was fulfilling an ancient promise to our people today. Sure, I explained, it was built on what had happened in the past, but God was inviting us to be a new kind of people. People filled with God's presence are able to be Jesus's people in and with the whole world. It must have been God, because it made sense, and the crowd hushed to silence. Then, someone yelled out, "Hey, what should we do about it?"

I told them the first thing that came into my head: "Repent and be baptized, every one of you, in the name of Jesus Christ for the forgiveness of your sins. And you will receive the Holy Spirit. The promise is for you and your children and for all who are far off—for all whom the Lord our God calls." I knew they could have what we had, but they needed to receive this Holy Spirit. I kept at them, warning them, too, about missing out and being stuck with the old, bankrupt ways of living.

That day people from all walks of life did what God asked them to do through me, and we baptized around 3,000 people. As they left their old selves behind, out of the river came a new movement—a movement that would change the world, a movement empowered by God's Spirit to see God's reign come on earth as in heaven.

✝

Prayerfully reflect on the wonders of the birth of the church in Acts 1–2 in light of this dramatization.

The Bible's Call: The Early Church and Poverty

The book of Acts and the epistle of James focus on being the alternate community of the kingdom of God. The resources that Christians have been given to fight and end poverty are described and outlined below.

Some Christian distinctives and poverty (Acts 2:42–47)

After the day of Pentecost, described in the reflection above, amazing things happened, not least of which was the hope of the kingdom being transformed into a movement, Christ's new body. There are three distinctive characteristics of the early church that we can see immediately after Pentecost that provide uniquely Christian responses to ending poverty.

The first passage to consider is Acts 2:42–47. What the Holy Spirit did was to animate the first disciples to live out the Christian life and stand together against poverty. Pentecost enabled ordinary people not to have to live under oppression, but rather be empowered to create a new identity and belonging. Whereas previously the poor were only eaten away by despair, the Holy Spirit filled them up with the hope to live as God's family, come what may. There have been ideological factions in Christ's body that deny or forget aspects of Pentecost. The fullness of the Spirit has been restricted because it didn't fit the emphasis or values of a particular denomination or church. The world's poor, however, can't afford this disunity or such blinders—they need the whole gospel. The world's poor need Jesus's body to be expressed fully, as it was in the early church, as a truly evangelical, charismatic, and radical community and movement.

An evangelical church and poverty

One of the evidences that the Holy Spirit came upon the early church was that they "devoted themselves" to various evangelical—that is, of the good news—disciplines (Acts 2:42). They experienced the authority of Jesus in the way described and practiced by the best of the evangelical movement. These disciplines included being devoted to:

- "the apostles' teaching"—they weren't just trying to "master the text," but the Spirit enabled them to be mastered by it;
- "fellowship"—they shared their lives together, and were with each other most days;
- "the breaking of bread"—life was centered on what Jesus had done and continued to do among and through them, including sacrificing their lives;
- "the prayers"—they encountered the Lord personally together, and interceded for the vulnerable against demonic forces.

If the poor and non-poor alike are to have their very identities re-created, they need to find ways to experience God and find his will. This is what these evangelical disciplines did for the early church; they reframed the frameworks the world and the demonic had set for the poor and the non-poor. For example, where the world declared the poor to be worthless, disciplines such as communion and teaching about what Jesus said created insight into the importance of the poor in God's reign. Where the demonic preyed on the most vulnerable, prayer created a spiritual authority to resist the demonic powers that seek to kill, steal, and destroy; it even busted disciples out of jail at times (Acts 4:23–31).

It must be conceded that it is possible to make even these disciplines into magic formulas rather than life-giving authority to live by the Spirit. They "devoted themselves," seeking to know the will and heartbeat of the Lord, whom together they obeyed. They didn't simply use or experience these disciplines as a way of getting what they wanted. Evidence that the Holy Spirit was at work—and not simply a counterfeit—was that sacrificial responses to Jesus's lordship were found. These community "listening devices" didn't make life more comfortable but helped create and sustain the sacrifices and lives required to work toward ending oppression. These disciplines helped forge an identity and confidence that could not be shaken by all that was happening around them and against them. They surrendered to God in these practices. God, in turn, transformed who they saw themselves to be and who they were, with the Holy Spirit's authority working through them.

What is tragic to me is that the authority of these disciplines has often been lost. The disciplines have become kinds of rituals to get through, rather than revolutionary practices to change the world. There is a big difference between "ritual" and "reasons." In the BBC television series *Yes Minister,* there was an episode about a hospital that was considered to be the best-run in Europe. The staff and management were the happiest around, efficient and never stressed. It always came in under budget. They used all the latest management techniques, and staff all got bonuses at Christmas.

There was only one slight problem: it never had any patients! They were great at following the right methods and rituals, but had forgotten why they existed.

The challenge for us as evangelical communities is to reconsider our practices and methods and remember why we do them. Preaching, praying, sharing communion, building community—these should not be empty rituals, but means to be receptive to God's will and initiative in our community life. How else will we know what initiatives God is taking with us that he has never taken before? Do we want to see new responses, or are we happy with the way things are and not interested in change? Will we allow God to raise up new methods of reaching people and changing our neighborhoods and societies? If we do, then we have to find again the reasons for many of our evangelical practices.

When was the last time you undertook some of these good news disciplines and surrendered with a group of people to doing what came of it? If we are to forge a new identity together, and resist the temptation of the world and the demonic, we need to be a truly evangelical community.

A charismatic church and poverty

The Holy Spirit invaded and informed the early church's areas of concern, especially through those without the world's power. Here were ordinary, unschooled people who had been with Jesus. They saw and heard things only God could do through these people. The society around this church experienced Jesus's interventions through a community that was responsive to God's authority in their daily lives. Evidence that the Spirit was at work included:

- they spoke in tongues (Acts 2:4): it was as if they were drunk—they lost any pretense for a respectable image, and let go of their own egos;
- awe came upon them (Acts 2:43): they experienced a sense of who God was, and his opinion of them mattered most;
- many signs and wonders were done (Acts 2:43): they saw lives changed as evidence of God's will being done on earth as in heaven.

The early church was animated by the Spirit to be the best of what the modern charismatic community has to offer. Ray Bakke once quipped that "the liberation theologians had a preferential option for the poor, but the poor had a preferential option for the

Pentecostals." Certainly, the growth of charismatic and Pentecostal churches amongst the world's poor can't be denied. In my experience, if there is a church based in a slum, it will nearly always be Pentecostal or charismatic. I wonder if a reason for this is an openness to the Spirit's work through ordinary people. God can quickly, in unusual ways, use ordinary people and is not limited to working through intellectual, highly educated leaders. "Be open and the Spirit can work through anyone, even me," they experience firsthand. In these slum churches everyone can participate because everyone has gifts of the Spirit to share with others. Certainly, this was part of the genius in the Azusa Street revival around the beginning of the twentieth century. This founding experience of the Pentecostal movement happened as an African-American preacher called people from all races to experience the day of Pentecost again in a poor part of Los Angeles. It spread throughout the world and is now the fastest-growing Christian movement today.

As the charismatic and Pentecostal wing of the church grows, though, it seems to be seeking more respectability. The recent move into right-wing politics, grand auditoriums, and celebrity leadership betrays its roots as a movement among the poor. Perhaps this is the inevitable life cycle from a movement to a monument of what it once stood for. Many of the evangelical movements that began in the nineteenth century experienced this institutionalization and are now in steep decline. Yet, this gaining of respectability and power by the charismatic church could be a huge loss to the poor. Indeed, it could be the beginning of the end, and the Spirit could move to more open groups, doing something new . . . again.

When was the last time we stepped away from our image-making so that the Spirit could use us in the ways only the Spirit can? If we are going to end poverty, we need the Spirit's gifts in each of us to be used. We must step out in these ways and be a truly charismatic community.

A radical church and poverty

At Pentecost the early church was empowered by the Spirit to be a truly radical community. One of the evidences of the Spirit's

143

coming was that a group of ordinary people became a truly radical community, able to go to the roots of both true faith and the reasons for society's problems. They found a way to surrender to God in faithfulness and relevance. Here are some of the evidences of this in the early church. The early Christians:

- were together—the Spirit enabled them to share life together;
- held all things in common—they shared what they had, beyond egos and claims of ownership;
- sold their possessions and goods—they surrendered all that gave false identities;
- distributed those possessions and goods to all as any had need—they shared belongings and found a way to redistribute wealth to those most in need;
- ensured no one was in need—poverty and injustice were defeated.

What the early church did has inspired people of faith for almost two thousand years. They modeled a way to live that called into question the ways of the dominant culture. They freely redistributed their wealth through the authority of the Spirit. They proved that it is possible for a community to live and keep living like Jesus if it surrenders to the power of the Spirit. What the rich young ruler could not do was done by ordinary people. The temptations resisted by Jesus can be resisted by us. Oppression and poverty can be ended with a taste of the kingdom. What inspires me today is that the same Spirit that took a scared group of disciples clinging on tightly to their securities, and transformed them into agents of change in the world, can do the same thing again.

I love being around radicals. There's a passion and a feistiness that is indomitable. While my roots are in the evangelical and charismatic church, I am a convert to the radical discipleship movement and long to see this tradition renewed. Writers, teachers, and preachers such as Athol Gill, John Smith, John Uren, Daryl Gardiner, and Mick Duncan have been rabbis to me, showing me the biblical ropes and helping me to obey Jesus above all else. Yet, even with the "emerging church" carrying the baton for a new generation in some ways, I doubt that many radicals today realize the seeds of revolution that are in their midst.

One source of deep regret is the constant loss of community experiments by Protestant radicals after short periods of time. We've been great at prophetic announcements, critiquing what is wrong with our church and society, but we have had real trouble building communities that last long enough to see transformation occur. I have written extensively elsewhere about the need for broad-based discipleship movements as well as tighter, more specialist apostolic communities. *Collective Witness*, *Sub-Merge*, and *Surrender All* called for a return to early church structures that enable specialist "apostolic" communities to be related, given space, and supported to live out their gifts within broader church structures. These kinds of communities are almost second nature to Catholic structures with their various kinds of orders, congregations, and parishes. However, it is almost always the cause of argument and schism within Protestant ones. If we are to end poverty, we need Protestants to create specialist communities able to live out the gospel in radical, sustainable, and innovative ways without trying to be everything for everyone. Such communities can spark and support the kind of radical Christian movement required to change neighborhoods and communities, and create new Pentecostal living for the multitudes. With which people will we risk our surrender? Will we be diligent in focusing more on being faithful as God's people with the poor rather than being "relevant"?

WWJDAP? (What Would Jesus Do About Poverty?) The Impact of the Early Church on Poverty (Acts 4:32–35)

The way personified by Jesus, his first community, and the early church movement worked. It was able to survive and thrive even though Jesus was with them in a different way after his execution.

> Now the whole group of those who believed were of one heart and soul, and no one claimed private ownership of any possessions, but everything they owned was held in common. With great power the apostles gave their testimony to the resurrection of the Lord Jesus, and great grace was upon them all. There was not a needy person among them, for as many as owned lands or houses sold them and brought the proceeds of what was sold. They laid it at the apostles' feet, and it was distributed to each as any had need.
>
> Acts 4:32–35

There was not a needy person among them! Such was the Jesus movement that poverty was ended in a group made up of many needy people. The Christian response to poverty, then, can be varied. Using the analogy of "fishing," consider that Jesus and the early church:

- gave fish—as when they responded to direct needs through healing or feeding the hungry. Today we could call this "relief," which could include responses such as feeding programs, emergency development, health care, prayer, providing accommodation, and visitation of those who are in jail or sick;
- taught people how to fish—as when they taught truths for people such as Zacchaeus to put into practice. Today we could call this "education," which could include responses such as job creation, preventative medical care, teaching literacy and numeracy, and vocational training;
- asked why there were no fish—as Jesus did when he turned the tables upside-down in the temple, or the apostles did when they confronted rulers and crowds who were oppressing people. Today we could call this "protest and advocacy," which could include addressing political systems, campaigning, and changing laws that create poverty and oppression.

Advocating population control and secure land tenure, and fighting unjust economic structures could also be included here;

- modeled a new way to fish—as Jesus did when he became human, forming an apostolic community living in solidarity, "fleshing out" good news with those in need. The apostles lived similarly, serving in weakness. This could be called "incarnational modeling," which could include responses such as Christians relocating to live among needy neighborhoods, the starting of neighborhood churches of the people, and life-on-life discipleship with those in need;

- saw a new way to fish, owned by the people—as Jesus and the apostles did when they so empowered a local movement that it could live on without them being physically there. Today we could call this "transformation," which could include neighborhood transformations, church planting movements of the poor, and grassroots Christian political cells.

Responding to poverty with relief or education can give us places to start. Each response is pleasing to God in its own right and can help in the move toward freedom from oppression. If these responses are to be like those of Christ and the early church, they cannot just be "bait" to catch fish. God wants to help restore the image of God in people, regardless of whether they acknowledge him or not. Responses to poverty, then, are not simply a means to the end of conversion or church growth. If our responses are not genuine, the poor will know it—they need to have finely tuned "B-S detectors" just to survive! So the poor might play the game for a while—"rice Christians" might even be made—but the deep-seated feelings of exploitation and resentment will be harder to shake. Credibility for Christ in the community might even be permanently damaged for some. Different kinds of responses to poverty can be blessed by God if they are done at the right time, in the right way, and with the right motivations. We know this because of the example of Jesus and the early church. Yet, if we ask, "Which of these responses to poverty do today's churches use most and least if they do get involved with the poor?" we are faced with some embarrassing answers. Despite the fact that Jesus and the early church did all these things, too often Christians are not prepared to go past relief. Why?

Perhaps the call to live among the poor to see a liberating Christian neighborhood movement is simply more costly and less sexy. It is one thing to feed the hungry; it is another to go to jail defending people's right to eat. With relief we can feel good about giving, but with transformation we have far more at stake than spare cash. It is hard to go past power as a motivation to stay in relief. In relief we are totally in control. By the time we see a transforming movement emerge, we who may initiate it are out of control.

With respect to the last two points above, the body of Christ has something unique to offer the world. Jesus and the apostolic bands showed the poor and those in solidarity with the poor "a new way to fish." Neighborhoods can gather together as a social movement to end poverty as we know it by following Jesus in the authority of the Holy Spirit.

Some of the biggest thrills I have had in mission are seeing pilot projects or new churches taken over by those who were helped by them. It is always a thrill for me to visit the Emmanuel Fellowship, which meets in a Scout hall in a suburb of Melbourne. When I see Simon preaching and leading the fellowship, I get a buzz. It brings back memories of when Simon was struggling; we would go fishing, talk about life, pray, and dream. Seeing converts run churches, no longer needing you—and in fact challenging and ministering to you—warms my heart like nothing else does.

Yet, with transformation of others came lack of control for me. I was once told that "a truly indigenous church is the one the missionaries hate"! I am not sure that is always the case! Yet, having trouble letting go is a very real temptation, especially if converts run things in a way that makes me cringe. Given that communities facing poverty often struggle to analyze their situations, I find it hard to shut up and allow the people to go through the process of learning without my input. This was especially the case when televangelists started filling our community with ideas of "prosperity and blessing being what you own." Yet, when a church is autonomous from us, we can only dialogue, not order. Our authority is more prophetic and medicine man-like than structural and chief-like. God has made these local leaders responsible for the project or church, after all, and not me. We have to trust that the Bible and Holy Spirit can guide them as they have guided us. This is not foolproof, but it does promote maturity, and allows a true movement of the people to emerge that can be God's answer to the cries of their hearts.

The first thing that almost always happens to those who are being transformed is a kind of independence. Input soon comes from elsewhere. This natural kind of maturing process—not unlike adolescence—is crucial if we are to work ourselves out of a job. Sure, they will make wrong calls. Yet, it is better for them to make the wrong calls than for those non-indigenous to the community to make the wrong calls. Ultimately, non-indigenous people can choose to walk away. Indigenous people don't have such power. It is crucial, therefore, that we aim to have the new way to fish be owned by the people.

While we may start with relief, we can't end there. What would Jesus do about poverty? He would take seriously every possible opportunity to see the good news proclaimed to and with the poor, especially when distinctly Christian movements stand against poverty together.

James and Fighting Oppression at a Community Level

It would be a mistake to focus only on Acts in this study of the early church and poverty. We will discuss at length the epistles of Paul in the next chapter, but here I want us to include some insights from James, addressed to one of the early churches belonging to the Acts tradition.

What God's reign does is have eternity break into the present. It is "already" true that those facing poverty are made in God's image and that those responsible for marring this are judged by God. Yet, this is "not yet" fully completed. James warns about this reality in stark terms.

> Come now, you rich people, weep and wail for the miseries that are coming to you. Your riches have rotted, and your clothes are moth-eaten. Your gold and silver have rusted, and their rust will be evidence against you, and it will eat your flesh like fire. You have laid up treasure for the last days. Listen! The wages of the laborers who mowed your fields, which you kept back by fraud, cry out, and the cries of the harvesters have reached the ears of the Lord of hosts. You have lived on the earth in luxury and in pleasure; you have fattened your hearts in a day of slaughter. You have condemned and murdered the righteous one, who does not resist you.
>
> Be patient, therefore, beloved, until the coming of the Lord. The farmer waits for the precious crop from the earth, being patient with it until it receives the early and the late rains. You also must be patient. Strengthen your hearts, for the coming of the Lord is near.
>
> James 5:1–8

Poverty disempowers people and communities, making them victims of injustice. Since God is just, he has a priority for those facing injustice. If we are to follow the Lord together, then the poor must become our priority, too. Will our churches identify the poor as central to God?

How, then, do the non-poor and poor find their solidarity together and find their new identities? In the New Testament the remedy for false identity is discipleship and community. This sense of belonging can help poor and non-poor alike to live as God intends and resist the temptations of false identities.

The body of Christ is to be the firstfruits of God's reign. It is not the same as God's reign, but should be the visible expression of it, demonstrating to neighbors what is eternal, being a role model of what God's reign is all about. It is also not the same as a nation-state, for it seeks to be a voluntary movement, showing the broader society what is possible with God. This is why some of Scripture's harshest sayings are reserved for when God's people do not reflect this reality. James writes,

> Religion that is pure and undefiled before God, the Father, is this: to care for orphans and widows in their distress, and to keep oneself unstained by the world. My brothers and sisters, do you with your acts of favoritism really believe in our glorious Lord Jesus Christ? For if a person with gold rings and in fine clothes comes into your assembly, and if a poor person in dirty clothes also comes in, and if you take notice of the one wearing the fine clothes and say, "Have a seat here, please," while to the one who is poor you say, "Stand there," or, "Sit at my feet," have you not made distinctions among yourselves, and become judges with evil thoughts? Listen, my beloved brothers and sisters. Has not God chosen the poor in the world to be rich in faith and to be heirs of the kingdom that he has promised to those who love him? But you have dishonored the poor. Is it not the rich who oppress you? Is it not they who drag you into court? Is it not they who blaspheme the excellent name that was invoked over you? You do well if you really fulfill the royal law according to the scripture, "You shall love your neighbor as yourself." But if you show partiality, you commit sin and are convicted by the law as transgressors.
>
> James 1:27–2:8

How can we follow such teachings in a global age? What does it mean to "love our neighbor as ourselves" when we can see our global neighbors suffering every night on our television sets and can make an instant response via the internet if we so choose? In such an age solidarity should be a key theme in following Jesus for those of us who are non-poor. It speaks of standing with the poor, not just deciding what to do for them. It speaks of joining our lives together to fight injustice, to have a stake in a common future together. In *The Brothers Karamazov*, Dostoyevsky's character Ivan says to Alyosha Karamazov, "One can love one's neighbors in the abstract or even at a distance, but at close range it's almost impossible" (263). Ivan is wrong. For becoming true neighbors— relocating our home to where most people live, especially those most in need—is the most glorious life a human being can live. With all the risks and inconveniences associated with such love, humans can touch the divine desire and be made alive. As Jesus explained to the disciples after the rich young ruler turned his back on the invitation to discipleship, "What is impossible with humans is possible with God."

Can we be inspired to love God and neighbor afresh, not in the abstract, but by taking up Jesus's invitation to enter the reality of human mess and suffering? Our future is tied up in the dreams of *shalom*, making a contribution, and living a meaning-full life. Such a life may seem temporally insane, but it is eternally significant. Perhaps a slum is a better place than most for my daughter Amy to have the opportunity for Paul's prayer for the Colossians to be answered—to be "filled with the knowledge of God's will in all spiritual wisdom and understanding, so that you may lead lives worthy of the Lord, fully pleasing to him, as you bear fruit in every good work and as you grow in the knowledge of God" (Col. 1:9–10).

To do what Jesus and the early church did about poverty requires us to find our identity, support, and inspiration at a personal and a collective level. In the New Testament, we see discipling relationships as a foundational way of sharing life with others and finding and living out this new identity in Christ. Jesus with the disciples, Paul with Timothy, and Barnabas with John Mark are just some examples. What is crucial here for those who want to take poverty personally is that we must take discipleship personally, too. We need to engage in life-sharing relationships. Indeed, unless we can find and develop these discipling relationships, everything else we want to see happen will not have the people to do it. In a very real sense the "resource engine" for any adventure in transformation is found in these kinds of personal relationships.

At a collective level there need to be discipleship movements among and in solidarity with the poor. Such movements do not just happen. They need a specialized community able to start and support them. This has been the story of the church throughout the ages. Can it be our story again today as we seek to end oppression?

Personal Reflection: Not Acts Again!

"Please open up your Bibles to Acts chapter nineteen," Pastor Suwot announced. This was no surprise. I had been part of the Ta Rua church for nearly four years, and every Sunday so far Pastor Suwot had preached from Acts. He'd take a line or phrase and speak for well over an hour exhorting and joking and telling all kinds of stories reminding us that this could happen again here in Klong Toey.

Of course, you can have too much of a good thing, so when I finally got to give sermons once a month at Ta Rua church, I wanted to broaden the base—Old Testament stories, Gospel stories, and even Paul. One month, however, I was desperately disorganized and went through my old sermon notes wanting to get one "ready, off the rack" to preach the next day. It was then I realized that most of my sermons to churches in Australia advocated discipleship amongst the poor. Not to be fazed, I preached from one of the Gospel passages, Matthew 25:31ff. (the sheep and the goats). The response, however, seemed odd. The congregation was with me, but few would make eye contact. There were no "Hallelujahs," as per normal. Surely, this difficult Gospel story was one all had to face up to. What was going on here?

No doubt, there was the dynamic of a white guy talking about poverty, something this community experienced every day of their lives, but there seemed more to it. This community needed a different message from those I was used to giving to the non-poor—a message of empowerment. It no longer surprises me that poor churches the world over look to Acts for their inspiration. The Pentecostal churches are some of the few churches making inroads into urban slums. They thrive on the hope of living out Acts again, offering the authority of the Spirit freely to all who come to Jesus. Pastor Suwot preaching every sermon on Acts and the Spirit's empowerment makes sense in difficult places. The early church was just like the Ta Rua congregation, ordinary people who had been with Jesus. They faced similar battles, drew from the Hebrew tradition in this light, and could do amazing things about their plight together in the power of the Spirit.

There is a perception that the early church of Acts did not address issues of poverty the way the Old Testament and the Gospels do. David Bosch, the late missiologist from South Africa, for example, writes:

> Whereas no serious student of Luke can doubt that the motif of the gospel as good news for the poor is absolutely crucial for the understanding of his gospel, it is equally obvious that this motif appears to have run dry in the Book of Acts.
>
> Bosch, *Transforming Mission*, 104

To be fair, Bosch goes on to explain that the idea of "salvation" in Acts includes addressing poverty and injustice, but here we note that themes of "the poor" and "poverty" are not taken up in Acts with the same intensity as in the Gospels.

Why would that be? Some may argue that after Jesus, the early church forgot the poor, were upwardly mobile, and no longer wanted to offend the rich as Jesus did. My explanation came to me when trying not to preach on Acts at the Ta Rua church. The early church, while composed of all kinds of classes and races, was predominantly a church of the poor. You simply don't need to preach about the poor to those who are already poor. Such a movement needs to be reminded that God offers his Spirit to ordinary people and that extraordinary things can happen, even in the most grim circumstances. Surely, this kind of hope is what the Christian faith has to offer those facing poverty. If his sermons are any indication, it's certainly Pastor Suwot's belief.

Maybe next month I'll take my sermon from Acts!

Questions for Discussion

- What most inspires you about the early church's responses to poverty? How do you experience it differently in today's church?
- From the way of Jesus and the early church, what do you see as the biggest contribution Christians can make to ending poverty?
- With which of the evangelical, charismatic, or radical wings of the church do you most relate? What do you see as the strengths and weaknesses of your tradition's role in ending poverty?
- What is the difference between the church and a national or state government? How are they related? Why do these differences and relationships need to be respected if Christians are to make a unique contribution to ending poverty?
- What can your faith community do to help end poverty together?

A Personal Exercise: Early Church Poverty Inventory

Take an inventory about how your experiences of Christian community stack up with the early church's responses to poverty. Which practices have you experienced, and which haven't you experienced? Why is this so? Find a way to gain an experience that you haven't had before of one of the practices of the early church life that responds to poverty.

Evangelical practices

- "Teaching of the apostles"—the people in Acts weren't just trying to "master the text," but the Spirit enabled them be mastered by it.
- "Fellowship"—they shared their lives together, and were with each other most days.

155

- "The breaking of bread"—life was centered on what Jesus had done and continued to do among and through them, including sacrificing their lives.
- "The prayers"—they encountered the Lord personally together and interceded for the vulnerable against demonic forces.

Charismatic practices

- They spoke in tongues, as though they were drunk—they lost any pretense for a respectable image, and let go of their own egos.
- "Awe came upon everyone"—they experienced a sense of who God was, and his opinion of them mattered most.
- "Many signs and wonders were done"—they saw lives changed as evidence of God's will being done on earth as in heaven.

Radical practices

- "They were together"—the Spirit enabled them to share life together.
- "They held all things in common"—they shared what they had, beyond egos and claims of ownership.
- "They sold their possessions and goods"—they surrendered all that gave false identities.
- "They distributed [these possessions and goods] to all as any had need"—they shared belongings and found a way to redistribute wealth to those most in need.
- "No one was in need"—poverty and injustice were defeated.

What would Jesus do about poverty? WWJDAP practices

- Give fish (relief, as Jesus did, with direct healing and feeding the hungry).

- Teach people how to fish (education and training, as Jesus did, teaching truths for people like Zacchaeus to put into practice).
- Ask why there are no fish (protest and advocacy, as Jesus did, turning the tables upside-down in the temple).
- Model a new way to fish (incarnational modeling, as Jesus did by becoming human, and living in solidarity with those he served).
- See a new way to fish, owned by the people (facilitating transformation, as Jesus did, empowering a movement and communities that can live on in the same way without us there).

7

Epistles

Letters from Jail and Other Tough Places of Discipleship

Opening Reflection: Paul in Jail

Paul was in jail when he wrote a letter to the Christian community in Philippi. In this letter there is one of the most insightful descriptions of the meaning of the Christian faith ever written. It is only a real God who can bring amazing life and inspiration from a dead-end place like a jail cell or a grave. As we have seen so far, in the midst of oppression, God takes a stand and uses people as instruments of change.

Jail conditions in first-century Palestine would have been harsh (perhaps not unlike some of the worst jails in Burma and Thailand). The first time I saw one of these cells was in Mae Sot, on the Thai-Burma border. It looked like it could have been stolen from the set of an old cowboy movie, with its vertical iron bars and a huge key dangling by the police officer's desk. But in this iron cage fifty people—mainly Burmese refugees and immigrant workers—were packed. All had to stand up, and the only place to go to the toilet was a bucket in the corner. The smell of sweat, urine, and feces was overpowering in the heat of that day. I had simply gone into the police station to ask for directions, but was quickly ushered out by embarrassed police officers. Over the years many of our Burmese, and more recently Thai, friends have suffered in such jails.

Anji says that the most chilling sound she has ever heard was the sound of leg irons clinking on the day she was in court for one of her Burmese friends. She shuddered when she turned to see a number of young Burmese, including a mother and her baby daughter, being brought in for their hearing.

(Read Philippians 1:12—2:13. Just try and imagine Paul writing about the nature of Christian faith from his jail, probably in leg irons, and probably in secret, by candlelight.)

According to Amnesty International (AI) the number of "prisoners of conscience" is almost impossible to figure. AI was launched as a call to stand in solidarity with those prisoners of conscience who had been forgotten. In 1945 the founding members of the United Nations approved the Universal Declaration of Human Rights. Two articles relate to "conscience."

> Article 18: Everyone has the right to freedom of thought, conscience and religion; this right includes freedom to change his religion or belief, and freedom, either alone or in company with others and in public or private, to manifest his religion or belief in teaching, practice, worship and observance.

> Article 19: Everyone has the right to freedom of opinion and expression; this right includes freedom to hold opinions without interference and to seek, receive and impart information and ideas through any media and regardless of frontiers.

The apostle Paul was denied these rights and was imprisoned, persecuted for his beliefs in ways similar to Burmese refugees. Locked up for putting their own convictions and commitments to others above their own safety and well-being, they faced torture, imprisonment, and even death.

The Bible's Call: From Difficult Places of Discipleship

The Christian faith is all about the real life that comes from sacrifice and commitment to others, and this has implications for those facing poverty today. This is what all Christians have to offer God. The apostle Paul and his Lord Jesus found ways to move beyond self-centered concerns and were amongst the most "others-centered" people that ever lived. In a self-centered age, they have much to teach us today. In this chapter we will look at two of Paul's epistles as we follow the theme of God's response to poverty.

Humility, Service, and Sacrifice in Philippians

From Paul's letter to the Philippians we will reflect on three aspects of the kind of faith that ends oppression. Paul, the well-educated Pharisee of the Pharisees who had oppressed and persecuted the vulnerable, including Christians, had been transformed. He lived a life of humility, service, and sacrifice and calls all people to this example.

Self-awareness: Putting our lives in perspective

Like Jesus and Paul we need to find a "humble" view of ourselves. In the eternal scheme of things, we are not that important. Any suffering we have been through helps in this regard. Imprisonment, or even illness or breakdowns, can make us alive to the truth of our vulnerability and smallness. These experiences help us find out what we are like and our own limitations.

Humility can be found anywhere—the view from a hilltop looking towards the coast, close friendships, and the mysterious joys that laughter brings. Often these make me feel there is so much more going on beyond my control or what I can generate. Yet when I find my own limitations, my sense of what I can and can't do is clearly seen.

Has any generation been better at avoiding limits? Today when we face real adversity we can always find music, books, TV, or movies to help avoid the sense that we have limits. Headache tablets, coffee, and energy drinks can keep us going when our body screams "enough!" We can e-mail everyone we know at once rather than spend face-to-face time with them. Mobile phones enable those we know to speak to us whenever they want. Dishwashers can take our dirty dishes and clean them in no time, giving us more family time—but family time is at an all-time low, time we used to spend washing and drying dishes together. All these "advances" should make our lives easier and enable us to do more. Yet, far too many of us have our worlds closing in on us. Like Gulliver in Lilliput, we tower over our tiny world, but don't see that we are being tied up. Our world has shrunk, and our self-importance is out of proportion to who we really are. Have we missed the chance to understand our miniature role in the history of the universe under the "advance" of technology?

If we are to make a difference among the poor, we have to look at the barriers each of us faces in making our contribution. While new technologies can make a sense of humility and self-awareness difficult, the underlying causes of our relentless drive for them are an important issue.

Perhaps we have an built-in drive toward status-seeking. We try to make ourselves look better or more important than others. If we are higher up the ladder of success, then others will accept us.

Even here in the slum you can see people going deep into debt, making massive sacrifices for the right clothes or the right telephone or the right motor scooter, even if they are expensive or unnecessary. Lotus and Carrefour shopping centers send their advertising leaflets into our slum and create the same insecurities here as elsewhere. Will our family be able to keep up with the next one? "If you don't have the right possessions, then you're not as important," seems to be the message.

Obviously, these pressures occur on a whole different scale in the West. How can CEOs justify a million-dollar-a-year package, or soccer players $100,000 a week to kick a ball? They could never spend this kind of money, even if they tried. Surely, there are only so many houses and cars and watches one can buy.

Why do so many fight so hard to gain salaries they could never spend in five lifetimes? The short answer is that if they are paid less than someone else in the company or the team, then they will be seen as having less value. Hence the need to be higher up on the status ladder, which is often measured by and tied to salary packages.

Most of us realize that to pin your worth to a dollar amount is shallow and not real in God's sight. Yet, this attitude has infiltrated churches and Christian organizations. Few "senior ministers" or "CEOs" are paid less than others in their organizations or churches, even if others have greater needs.

A hundred years ago, no one had TVs or radios beaming in thousands of advertisements a day. Now because of media bombardments and seeing firsthand what others have, most people on the planet think they are entitled to far more than they have.

We need to hear the apostle Paul's warning afresh, "Do nothing from selfish ambitions or conceit, but in humility consider others better than yourselves" (Phil. 2:3). In Paul's time most people assumed that they would stay at the same status as their parents. If their father was a carpenter, they would expect to be a carpenter. If a slave, then a slave. A ruler, then a ruler. Few envisaged jumping rungs of the social ladder.

As Alain de Botton's *Status Anxiety* has so rightly observed, few today are not scheming or making decisions based on climbing the ladder to the very top. And, of course, we have to say it is possible for some actually to do this. Athletes and pop stars are just some of the high-profile people who do this at a rapid rate.

While these changes in society can open great possibilities and few would want to return to pre-industrial fiefdoms, today's societies can also create an intense insecurity and unhappiness in us. If everyone can reach the top, then everyone is our competitor and most of us are failures. We can't even enjoy our peers doing well.

In the midst of these realities, can we seek a humble view of ourselves as human beings? To be humble is to have a right view or ourselves. There are two temptations in this.

First is the temptation of the poor. Too often the poor can believe they are less than human and will put up with maltreatment because they think they deserve it. It's their karma, or it's divine will, or it's their lot in this life. Suck it up and get used to it.

Yet, the God of the Bible says that every human being is made in the image of God, is a child of God, and deserves dignity and a full life. Read through Paul's letters to some of the poorest communities in the Roman Empire and hear what he says (for example, the first chapter of Ephesians).

A change in Christianity today is that many Christians question whether all people would benefit from a Christian identity. Isn't it oppressive to actively seek to change people's religious alliance and identity? After living where I do, I can only answer that the poor need a Christian identity more than most. It is the only way dignity can be fully restored and freedom gained from the slavery of karma and fate. In Christ people can be free and experience their intrinsic worth as God's sons and daughters.

Issues of religious identity are not necessarily the place to start conversations with our Buddhist neighbors. All kinds of issues often need to go before it in living out the good news. However, having a right view of ourselves as God's children and how Jesus can enable us to belong to his body is important for every human being. Refusing to raise issues of identity and belonging is to withhold a key resource in fighting poverty. Jesus is Lord of all or not Lord at all, and his acceptance of the "least of these" on the status ladder helps the poor see that they are of far more importance than most think they are.

Second is the temptation of the rich. The temptation of the rich is that of thinking they are gods. In a world of so much poverty, they think they can live as they want and decide who dies and who lives. Not many would describe themselves as rich, but in world terms most of those able to buy and read this book would fit into this category. You most probably have the power to decide how you spend your money today and who misses out on it. Many are dying because Christians will not share what they have.

It is also non-poor Christians who deprive the poor of an identity in Christ. Too often rich Christians think they have power over who the Lord God is and what God wants because they have the resources to choose. But, look at the way Jesus responded to the Pharisees and other rich rulers of the day in Matthew 23. The language couldn't be stronger. Whoever said Jesus didn't curse?

Those born into financial and religious privilege are simply human beings who are worth no more than others facing death. We are not gods. The good news is that we can be redeemed from our arrogance if we become part of the body of Christ with the world's poorest.

There are too many religious and financially spoiled kids. They simply don't want to share Christ or invite others to join this life because these people may have another faith. Yet, this takes for granted the sacrifices of past generations that made possible this identity "in Christ." Perhaps this is the root cause of thinking we are gods—we forget where we have come from. We forget that every Christian had somebody (themselves or an ancestor) risk themselves in crossing a religious barrier for the opportunity for an identity in Christ. For some this may have been in the time of the early church, but for others today this is yet to happen. If it is wrong to invite those who don't have this identity now, surely it was wrong then. If you don't believe in evangelism, to be consistent you should give up the faith and go back to your forebear's original religion! Perhaps, if you think you're a god who knows everything, you already have, but have just kept the title "Christian" for decoration or social acceptability.

It is time for rich Christians to give up telling God what God can and can't do. It doesn't make sense to me that people who have been liberated in Christ would want to deny this to others.

This is not to say that anybody, especially the poor, should be tricked, exploited, or coerced into becoming a Christian. For those who are rich, the way of resisting temptation is not to exert power, but to do some reality testing and serve in partnership with the poor. This need for reality testing and partnership is one of the reasons why three churches in Australia want to become sister churches with the Ta Rua church here in Klong Toey. They don't want just to keep on living for themselves, consuming what they have and taking it for granted, but to stand with a slum church and all the challenges they face. Through Ta Rua these churches can see the way the world really is and what they have to offer. This is one of the gifts Ta Rua is to the world. It is not an easy journey together, but in humility we can consider others better than ourselves, and become others-centered and true to the Christian faith, coming to terms with our own limitations and graces.

Authentic service

The way to love and meaning is the way of Jesus: committing all we have to the well-being of others with whom we are in solidarity. Jesus is, of course, the great example. Paul says we should have the "mind of Christ" who "emptied himself" so that he could give himself totally to God in serving others.

The Greek words for the words "servant" and "empty" do not translate well into English. The word *doulos* means something more like becoming a slave for others; *kenos* means something more like having nothing left. Jesus did this for us, and Paul says the way of the Christian faith is to follow Jesus in this direction.

This can sound oppressive or even psychologically unhealthy to some. Yet, the way of authentic serving—rather than controlling—is the way that makes the ultimate difference in our lives and the lives of others. I think it is the key to the Christian's response to poverty, too, for in doing so we let go of our own egos and let God direct our responses with others.

We can have wrong views of ourselves and impure motivations in the ways we respond to those in need. For example, some

165

people will give offerings so that they will get money or kudos back. Some Christians even treat God like this. But this is not true faith. True faith is about surrendering all to God so that God will do through us what God wants. We have to embrace the idea of emptying ourselves and serving.

One of my heroes in serving is Ajan Suwot. Although he came from a mafia and drug-addict background, he came to faith and now is as healthy and dynamic a person as you could meet. He could easily choose to move his family out of the slum and go to another, nicer part of Thailand. He is an amazing preacher and visionary and would not be out of place as pastor of a big church somewhere. In fact, for a time he planted a church outside the slum in another part of Thailand. But he chose to come back with his family to Klong Toey and has served our community here in big and small ways every day for the last fourteen years.

Most of Suwot's surrendering to and serving God is unseen, except by God. But I see the way my neighbors respect him when he visits us. I see the way soccer players appreciate the time he takes to support them and organize camps for them. I see how exhausted he is after soccer practice on Saturday mornings, and while I'm ready to collapse in a heap, I know that in the afternoon Suwot will take another group of young people out to play ping-pong. The whole neighborhood would have stories of seeing Ajan Suwot doing what is humanly impossible, and experiencing him as a channel of God's love and grace.

This emptying and serving deeply challenges me. Can my life be a channel of God's love and peace, too? Will I have faith in God and not just try to use God to get what I want? Will I be an authentic servant of Jesus and not just do what will be seen by others?

Suffering, the hope of heaven, and Christ's love

Jesus served others so much that he was killed. Why? Because of the way he lived. His service was not magic, but an example of true faith. That's why Paul was in jail, too, when he wrote this

166

letter to us. "Becoming obedient to the point of death," Paul wrote of Jesus, and could have written of himself.

Is it true that because of my identity in Christ I could be killed by serving the poor, too? The short answer is that if you follow Jesus's life you, too, may also follow Jesus's death. This is my problem with Mel Gibson's *The Passion of the Christ*. When Amy, my daughter, was eight years old, she walked in on us watching the movie. It's not a kids' movie, but she saw the torture scenes and asked why the people killed Jesus. The movie doesn't answer this question.

Jesus didn't hide this aspect of the Christian life. He said, "Deny yourself, take up your cross and follow me." Matthew 10:16–25 talks about this clearly. If we step out as disciples of Jesus to help end oppression, what can we really expect of God in return? What can we trust God for when we are seeking the well-being of others?

We live in the in-between times of God's reign, a time of war, where there are casualties. God's will is being done on earth as in heaven, but it is not completed yet. This will end and Jesus will win, but for now the battle rages on between the demonic, the flesh, and the world on one side and God's forces on the other. In this battle, we must acknowledge that many of God's greatest servants risked everything for Jesus and were not protected from death.

In June 2004 UNOH had its first "Surrender" conference. While Tony Campolo was the headline speaker, it was Mick Duncan who caused the controversy. Mick shared some of the places he had been in discipleship. They were some dark places, indeed: living in a slum in Manila that was burned down, rejection by other Christians, and the loss of his child Joseph. If anyone has the right to ask, "What can we really trust God for?" it is Mick. His answers, however, were not comfortable ones. We even had people praying against Mick at the back of the auditorium in some of his later sessions.

Mick's conclusions were simple. In a time of war, where the battle is real, we can only really trust that:

- God loves us;
- one day we will be with God in heaven.

(Mick has now expanded and published these reflections in a book entitled *Who Stands Fast? Discipleship in Difficult Places.* I recommend it to you.)

Mick is right. We need an eternal perspective if we are to have a right view of ourselves and our service of others. While the forces of evil can hurt us, death is not the end. Jesus's death was not the end. He rose again so that we could, too.

Mick implores us to consider the role of prayer in this war zone. He writes,

> It has often been said that prayer is a means by which God can influence us, but in the Moses moment we see a prayer influencing God. Possibly this is what John Wesley had in mind when he said: "God will do nothing but in answer to prayer." Without wanting to suggest that everything hinges upon our prayer life, Walter Wink is right to suggest that "God's hands are effectively tied when we fail to pray." So, in a very real sense the future is ours to create. We do have what Gregory Boyd refers to as "say-so" in this world. God will not always unilaterally determine all things and waits for us to influence him through our prayers.
>
> Duncan, *Who Stands Fast?*

Prayer clears the way for God to do his work in the war zone of oppression. We can't rely on our own abilities here, only God's intervention. Paul would later write, "Pray in the Spirit at all times in every prayer and supplication. To that end keep alert and always persevere in supplication for all the saints. Pray also for me, so that when I speak, a message may be given to me to make known with boldness the mystery of the gospel, for which I am an ambassador in chains. Pray that I may declare it boldly, as I must speak" (Eph. 6:18–20). If Paul needed such intercession, how much more will those of us who are far less gifted or courageous?

Of course, Tony Campolo can never be outdone. He provided some great insights about true serving and the way of the cross.

The way of humility is not the way of more titles, he argued, but more testimonies. He once did an amazing impersonation of his African-American pastor at a graduation service: "Pharaoh—had the title. Pharaoh. Now that's a great title. An important title. But Moses, he had the testimooooony!" The titles we earn from education, employment, or fame will not make a lasting impact in a world of poverty. But the testimonies of those whose lives we have impacted will live on.

Any short-term cost to us should be counted a privilege. Paul explains: "Therefore God also highly exalted him and gave him the name that is above every name, so that at the name of Jesus every knee should bend, in heaven and on earth and under the earth, and every tongue should confess that Jesus Christ is Lord, to the glory of God the Father" (Phil. 2:9–11). Is God's love and hope of heaven enough for us? Are we prepared to live a life that will have an eternal impact by standing with the poor, come what may? A life that will live on long after we're gone? This is the inspiration of the Christian faith and what it has to offer in ending poverty: life is short, so serve and pray hard!

The Corinthian Community: Reflections on Foolishness

There is no way to be both cool and in solidarity with the poor. This is a strong theme with Paul, as we see in his letters to the Corinthian church. For example, Paul writes:

> For the message about the cross is foolishness to those who are perishing, but to us who are being saved it is the power of God. For it is written, "I will destroy the wisdom of the wise, and the discernment of the discerning I will thwart." Where is the one who is wise? Where is the scribe? Where is the debater of this age? Has not God made foolish the wisdom of the world? For since, in the wisdom of God, the world did not know God through wisdom, God decided, through the foolishness of our proclamation, to save those who believe. For Jews demand signs and Greeks desire wisdom, but we proclaim Christ crucified, a stumbling block to

Jews and foolishness to Gentiles, but to those who are the called, both Jews and Greeks, Christ the power of God and the wisdom of God. For God's foolishness is wiser than human wisdom, and God's weakness is stronger than human strength.

Consider your own call, brothers and sisters: not many of you were wise by human standards, not many were powerful, not many were of noble birth. But God chose what is foolish in the world to shame the wise; God chose what is weak in the world to shame the strong; God chose what is low and despised in the world, things that are not, to reduce to nothing things that are, so that no one might boast in the presence of God. He is the source of your life in Christ Jesus, who became for us wisdom from God, and righteousness and sanctification and redemption, in order that, as it is written, "Let the one who boasts, boast in the Lord."

1 Corinthians 1:18–31

When Christians talk of living out New Testament Christianity, the church in Corinth is not what most of us have in mind. Yet, its settings and struggles provide wisdom for us today if we are prepared to reconnect to its place and message. I can't help but make connections between Paul's experiences at Corinth and our own with the Rainbow Church in Melbourne.

A Christian community of the underside: Lifting up the margins

Corinth in Paul's day was a hub of activity. All traffic from the north to the south of Greece passed through Corinth of necessity, and the greater part of the east to west traffic of the Mediterranean passed through there by choice. The traffic in this port area meant that Corinth was a multicultural population, a place where the entire world met. Corinth had a reputation not only for commercial prosperity, but also for evil living, drunkenness, and debauchery. The church was in many ways a mirror of the city. First Corinthians 7:20–24 suggests that some were even slaves. The picture that emerges of Corinth is one of a community in which the majority was at the lower end of the socioeconomic ladder.

First Corinthians 12:13 explains how Corinth's diverse people—Jew, Greek, slave, free—are all one in Christ. Given the sociology of the day, this entailed a radical lifting up of the margins. There was a real underside to this city, but the gospel was taking root there. Paul explains in 1 Corinthians 1:26–31 that God chose them, the foolish of the world, to shame the wise.

Anji and I can relate to the setting of the church in Corinth. We lived for ten years in Springvale, an industrial suburb in the southeast of Melbourne. There were 140 different people groups represented there, 116 languages spoken at the local secondary college, and with its cultural diversity and richness it had become a place where people from all over the world were drawn together. There were refugees and asylum-seekers, people with mental illness, and those on low incomes. Springvale and nearby Noble Park also had a well-established reputation as a center of heroin activity. Rainbow Church, with its focus on those struggling with mental illness and addictions, also has its own fair share of struggles as it seeks to be an authentic Christian community open to "all the colors of the rainbow."

As with the church in Corinth, Rainbow is intentionally a mirror of its city. Within this context, Rainbow encourages people to recognize that they do not have to have all their problems sorted out for the journey of following Christ to begin.

Yet, when I see people from Rainbow struggle to their feet, try to explain why communion is so vital to their lives, and then encourage everyone to join in, I encounter a mystery beyond mere words. They have something to offer the world that comes directly from God. There is no pretense here, just a sharing of what helps them get through the day.

I can't help but compare these experiences with a recent encounter with a young Bible college student who raced up to me during a coffee break with panic in his eyes. He was in a class looking at the ways Mark's Gospel connects with contemporary society. He had just heard one of my Burmese friends tell his story of persecution and torture and was clearly shaken.

"A few of us [students] have been talking, and we are concerned about this course. It's just so troubling," the student said.

"What exactly troubles you about what you're hearing?" I asked.

"Oh, it's not what we are hearing. We don't know when assignments are supposed to be handed in. Is it next week or the week after? There seems to be a discrepancy."

The life and connections of the gospel are often missed by those "in the know," but often found intuitively by those on the underside, whose pain and dislocation draw them into God's reality. Will we give those on the underside the space to be heard, lifted up, and honored, as Paul calls the Corinthian church to do?

A human church

The Corinthian church was a very human church of Christ. It may not have been Paul's "pin-up" church, as there were reports of sexual immorality (1 Cor. 5:1) and members cheating on each other (1 Cor. 6:8). Yet, Paul does not write them off. He calls them "saints" (1 Cor. 1:2), seeing who they can be and calling them to the fullness of this identity in Christ. Genuine love can not only help us see the best in others, but also long for resolution of brokenness. Sin is tragedy, missing the mark of what people were made for, and Paul sought ways for the Corinthian discipleship community to move beyond the drama to follow Christ more closely.

In a similar way, with Rainbow we needed to learn to accept people where they were, but also be committed to their long-term well-being. The Rainbower who forgets to take medication, the one who goes back to the bottle, the one who loses reality and home in the confusion of both—standing with these people is different from the moralizing many of us were brought up to fear. All of us need to hear the challenge to follow Christ more closely amidst the voices that say the little things (to us) don't matter. Paul keeps reminding the Corinthian community that all our actions affect each other (1 Corinthians 12) and must be put under the lordship

172

of Christ. Are people secure enough in our love for them that we can challenge unhealthy behavior?

A vulnerable church

Paul struggled with legitimate—as well as crackpot—itinerants that destabilized the community at Corinth. Different teachers were coming through, and divisions emerged based on which teachers people followed (1 Cor. 1:12–14). Not committed to the community's long-term well-being, these teachers created chaos.

Christian communities can often get caught up with outside input. Whether it is the network marketing people offering the latest "get rich quick scheme" or a televangelist offering cheap grace and prosperity, many of us are suckers for shortcuts. "If we just get this latest thing, all will be well." Paul was willing to name the temptation of the instant by modeling and offering an alternative—long-term, sacrificial commitment to the community (1 Cor. 4:11–16). In the end, we have to trust that the Bible and the Holy Spirit will guide the Rainbow church, just as we believe we have been guided. Yet, to do this we must be in solidarity with Christian communities over the long-term, not in the impulse of the instant.

Over time people in Rainbow have been fooled by the bigger and the better. This is especially the case for those who have a great deal of healing in their lives and no longer want to be associated with the "fools" they used to be. Perhaps this is the greatest challenge to Rainbow Church: to live with vulnerability and not to try to hide or run away from it.

The Christian community in Corinth was not a picture-perfect community. It was, however, an authentic Christian community, one that experienced the risen Christ in the midst of real life. It provides a model for those in poor communities. We need more such communities today if the lost and poor are to be reached and oppression ended.

Paul calls for foolishness. To stand against the dominant, demonic culture (represented in 1 Corinthians 8–10), given the predominance of idol worship in the day, would be considered crazy by the rest of the city. Yet, this risk of standing with the living Christ—regardless of public opinion or vested interests—was the challenge Paul called them to take.

Are we prepared to be a foolish church today? Perhaps standing against injustice with asylum-seekers, those suffering mental illness, or those with drug addictions is foolishness to 80 percent of the population; yet, it is a stand we must be prepared to take in seeking Christ's kingdom amongst the poor. Jesus said, "As you do it to one of the least of these . . . you do it to me" (Matt. 25:31ff.). Are we prepared to let him into our community life and stand with him, come what may?

Personal Reflection: How Beautiful Are Feet?

Sometimes I don't get Paul. He once wrote, "How beautiful are the feet of those who bring good news!" (Rom. 10:15). I mean, take a look at my feet! What kind of news must I be bringing?

Nearly everyone here in Kong Toey slum has feet like mine. Over time the combination of flip-flops on hot concrete transforms even the softest hooves into gross monsters able to scare small children at a single glance. Feet are a tell-tale sign of poverty here. If we ever go out of the slum with neighbors, say to a movie, it feels like people are staring us down and thinking, "Yeah, wear your best shirt if you like, but shuffling along on those flaky feet tells us exactly where you're from."

Compare our feet to the office workers', who rarely touch plastic and concrete as they get out of their air-conditioned offices into their air-conditioned cars back to their air-conditioned homes. Though it's 100°F outside, they all probably wear socks all day and night! Some even get professionals to massage, groom, and make their feet smell sweet!

I am encouraged that Jesus probably didn't have beautiful, sweet-smelling feet. Other than a borrowed donkey, he walked those dusty, dirty, first-century Palestinian streets on his speaking and healing tours. Certainly, the disciples didn't line up to take turns to wash each other's feet at the end of a long day's journey. Jesus's rough feet were finally disfigured by having a nail hammered through them. Not the kind of feet to show off down at the beach club.

Had Jesus lived like a televangelist on tour in the best private jets and swanky hotels, he would have had nice feet, but there would not be any good news for the poor. It was because his feet took him to the tough places, showing a new way to live, that the good news came. There is no other way to bring the gospel than to enflesh it. Jesus's life, death, and resurrection made the good news real for the poor, and his fleshy feet would have shown the marks.

If Jesus didn't have beautiful feet, neither did Paul. They lived remarkably tough lives, but brought the ultimate good news. What's this verse about feet really about, then? The Greek word gives us a clue. Translated as "beautiful" is *horairias*, which is actually closer in meaning to our word "timely" or the "right season" than "beautiful" or "extremely good-looking." It comes from the root that means "hour." The verse, then, is about feet bringing timely news, which in turn has an eternal beauty.

While my wife is beautiful in every sense, we have struggled to make our home in Klong Toey beautiful in every way. Anji wrote about this:

Over the time we have been here in the slum, I have been slowly fixing things up, or so I thought, to make the place more liveable.

When Aiden was four months old, we made a kind of kid's bedroom and put in a small air conditioner. To keep the air in, we had to block up many holes in the walls and windows, initially with plastic bags and then eventually with wood. Well, I thought I was pretty clever. Covering up the holes also meant a reduction in the number of mosquitoes that could get in. However, I was

175

soon to learn that many problems that look easy to solve here in the slum are not that simple!

Our house began to constantly stink like a public toilet! Ash's conclusion was, "It's a slum. Everything smells." I, however, was quite disconcerted that our house seemed to smell more than the outside sewer. I went on a mission with sprays and cleaning products, as well as poisons, to kill the various vermin that I suspected to be causing the strong smell. Well, nothing worked.

Then a month before we left for Australia, urine started leaking through the ceiling. One morning I was settling down to enjoy my morning cup, when wee started dripping through the roof into the kettle and splashing into my bowl of cereal. I decided that this rat was a goner!

We set traps and caught a number of rather large rats before leaving. After returning from Australia, I started to notice a really strong smell around 3:00 a.m. each morning. Then one day I woke up to a yellow puddle, much of which had splashed into my nearby handbag!

Hoping to set a rat trap upstairs, I asked our neighbor to help me with a light, which had broken. He pulled back the plastic sheet used to cover the rough wooden floor, and we found the wood completely soaked with urine. He determined that a rat couldn't make such a large quantity, so it must be human! Now I was ready to throw my kettle out!

Over the next few days his sister-in-law, who lives in one of the four rooms upstairs, decided to keep a lookout for the culprit. After two more puddles of urine, we discovered the 3:00 a.m. wee-er, a frail old man who can't manage the stairs down to the toilet very well at night. Well, now he has a bucket, which we have offered to empty each morning if he promises not to keep weeing on the floor! Soon I hope to start to open up some of the holes in the walls in a hope that airflow will help reduce the stink of urine-soaked, rotting wood.

Anyway, it got me to thinking about so many of the issues that we see in the slum, that look so easy to fix, but often leave us baffled as to why things are the way they are. I can be so guilty of rushing in with a quick fix that may just make things smell worse in the end! I pray that God will guide us as we try to listen more than talk, understand more than seeking to be understood, and work together with, rather than for, the poor in this community.

In a world of a billion urban slum dwellers, should timely feet end up ugly feet? Does it matter if our house doesn't make the front cover of *House Beautiful*? What becomes ugly now for the sake of the gospel—from poverty, hardship, crossing barriers—has a real kind of beauty from doing what counts for eternity. What is considered beautiful now in polite society is an ugly waste of time in eternity. Is it now the case that the uglier our feet, the better the news for us and a hurting, concrete-clad world?

By 2025 there will be two billion urban slum dwellers, so we could do with a few more Christian feet getting ugly to bring good news. C'mon, ugly feet, keep walk'n'!

Questions for Discussion

- What do you find most appealing and most disturbing about Paul?
- Do you agree with this quote about political prisoners? Why or why not?

  "Any movement that does not support its political internees is a movement destined to fail. When power is challenged, it inevitably turns to violent repression and imprisonment to maintain itself. In order to avoid defeat, movements must become organized and capable of combating the repression of the state apparatus, and they must be able to support their comrades and allies in the event that they are arrested or imprisoned."

- What belief or cause would you be willing to go to jail for? What wouldn't be worth it?
- Why is sacrifice required in order for poverty to end?

A Personal Exercise

Go to the Amnesty International website, www.amnesty.org, and find out about one political prisoner you could help. Make contact with AI—if possible, send a letter—and stand in solidarity with this prisoner of conscience. What would it mean for you to take your own conscience as seriously in ending poverty?

Apocalypse Now
Last Things and the Things That Last

Opening Reflection: John's End-of-Life Vision

John lay on his death bed and saw a vision that took seriously the nature of a fragile world. It was a broken and hurting world, which would keep going long after his last gasp of air. Most of the original apostles had been tortured, imprisoned, or killed at the hands of the fledgling discipleship movement's enemies by the time the book of the Revelation was written. John, however, finished his life in exile on the island of Patmos as an elderly man. John had suffered greatly for his love of others. Yet through it all, he had helped to start and support Christian discipleship movements, and this was his letter to them. It was something that would live on, well after his death.

Perhaps John's description of himself in the opening chapter of Revelation provides insights about what really lasts: "I, John, your brother who shares with you in Jesus the persecution and the king-dom and the patient endurance, was on the island called Patmos because of the word of God and the testimony of Jesus" (Rev. 1:9).

John is a brother in an eternal family that had already started and will last forever. This family is a great equalizer, where both poor and non-poor can belong. The fact that John was in exile rather than executed is probably a sign that he was from a wealthy family. He intentionally rejected this privilege, however, and chose to belong to a new family. This new family shared Jesus, who makes equality possible because of the life he lived.

This sharing of Jesus's life, however, is costly. John experienced persecution that required the same patient endurance that Jesus had. The hope of the kingdom was not fully realized yet, but the suffering and battle scars would not be in vain. To John and his supporters, it must have felt as though they were in retreat in the face of the power and prestige of the Roman Empire, an empire that crucified Jesus and exiled John. John was forced to the isolated island of Patmos, where he had a breathtaking vision of what was happening in the cosmos.

Being away from the empire, John saw with greater clarity. From the margin he could see what was happening in a way those at the center could not. Facing his own mortality, John had a final word from the Lord to the communities he loved and had served with his life.

Tony Campolo talks about a survey, completed by elderly people over eighty years old, that asked, "If you had to live your life again, what would you have done differently?" The responses were simple ones, really—they would have reflected more, taken more risks, or done more things that would live on after they died. Perhaps the elderly and exhausted John of Patmos is answering this question in his own way through the book of Revelation: What of value will really last?

(Prayerfully read through the letter to John's churches in Revelation 2–3.)

John seems to have had few regrets, but was clearly worried about those in whom he had invested his life. The vision then manifests itself in the weird and the wonderful, written in a kind of apocalyptic code. Yet it is a vision that indicates clearly what is worthwhile and what counts in a fragile world.

The Bible's Call: Resistance Is Use . . . full

Apocalyptic literature is found throughout the Bible, not just in the book of Revelation. In many ways Revelation is the New Testament equivalent to the book of Daniel in the Hebrew Bible. In the first six chapters of Daniel, we see Daniel as a new kind of Joseph. Then the book turns sharply, with Daniel having an amazing series of visions. Daniel especially draws on images from Jeremiah (31:31–34), Ezekiel (16), and Isaiah (2:2–4). The two books, Daniel and Revelation, have in common the fact that they are set in times of empire, when God's people are under another power's rule. This is where the genius of apocalyptic writing comes in. The secret codes help the resistance movement get their message out to inspire and inform without drawing unnecessary attention to themselves.

Jesus, especially in the first three Gospels, and Paul used apocalyptic images or a kind of heavenly code to get their messages out. The messages were for the true believers, or those wavering under the pressure of the empire. The fledgling Jesus movement needed cover from those in Rome's empire who were trying to destroy them and God's plan.

In the last century or so apocalyptic literature made a comeback. The Scofield Reference Bible made all kinds of claims about the future and predictions that these codes were supposed to reveal. This tradition was taken up with gusto in such books as Hal Lindsey's *The Late, Great Planet Earth* and more recently the *Left Behind* series by Tim LaHaye. These have scared witless millions of people over the last two generations principally by using apocalyptic images as a kind of predictor of future events. At best they can scare people into taking action, but at worst they can use apocalyptic literature as a kind of Christian version of Nostradamus or the zodiac.

What, then, is this apocalyptic literature? The best definition I have seen is from a book by Wes Howard-Brook and Anthony Gwyther called *Unveiling Empire: Reading Revelation Then and Now*. In it they define this kind of writing as "the world view that life takes place on two levels simultaneously: an 'earthly' level in which evil or Satan temporarily reigns over sinful humanity, and a 'heavenly' level in which God reigns: the 'heavenly' level is already victorious over the 'earthly' level" (4).

For our study of poverty, what is interesting about this kind of understanding of the Bible's "heavenly code" is that it speaks of the folly of investing and trusting in the temporal and what seems to be strong at any given "earthly" time. Perhaps this is why this style is employed by the writers—it is the best form of writing to convey the message of "no compromise" without getting caught. They can secretly—but in the strongest terms possible—call those tempted to give in to the power of "beasts" to stand firm. The empire may have the power to destroy the readers' lives now, but not in the eternal realm. The earthly riches that Babylon offers now are nothing compared to the riches to come in the New Jerusalem. In the eternal realm the pain now is nothing compared to the pain the oppressors will feel when temporal and eternal come together. John urges us to be on the right and just side of history.

Myth and Counter-myth

A key to understanding what Revelation has to say about poverty is to understand the myths of the dominant empire against which this book argues. It has been noted by scholars such as Peter Berger that the Roman Empire had a "sacred canopy" of assumptions that legitimized it. These are identified as empire, peace, victory, faith, and eternity. As we will see in this chapter, these myths cause and support poverty and oppression now as then. What John's Revelation does is expose these myths and outline a vision of what God will bring into being and has started already.

In the following discussion of these myths I especially have drawn from the excellent research of Howard-Brook and Gwyther.

Myth one: Whose empire?

An important Greek word to understand in Revelation's context is *basileia*. It is used often by Jesus in the Gospels and by John. It is generally translated as "kingdom" or "reign." Yet, this was also the primary way Rome described itself in the Greek-speaking world.

What John did, then, was subvert this phrase. By challenging the application of this term only to Rome, he called into question who is fit to rule the world. At the peak of Rome's power, early Christianity raised the provocative question of whom empire ultimately belongs to. Was it these tiny, scattered Christian discipleship movements, or was it the most powerful armed force then known? Those in John's day would have asked, Is this madness, treason, or both?

John's vision, however, is relentless in answering the question (Rev. 5:10; 12:10; 22:5). A good example of this is Revelation 11:15: "The kingdom [*basileia*] of this world has become the kingdom of our Lord . . . and he will reign [*basileusei*] forever and ever."

Where God's people resisted the Roman Empire, it ceased to reign over them. Such resistance turns the whole world "upside-down," or more accurately, "right-side up." For the ultimate authority and center is Jesus Christ. Living out what is true in the heavenlies is truer than what seems to be happening on earth.

In a time of globalized, free-trade agreements that are ushering in a new era of empire, what should be our response? Can we resist this market empire that, like Rome, could make our lives cheaper and easier, but exploit the most vulnerable at the same time? Surely, John's Revelation could have been written of today when it says, "No one can buy or sell who does not have the mark, that is, the name of the beast or the number of its name" (Rev. 13:17).

Participating in this empire is ultimately destructive. Its beneficiaries are liable for the judgment: "A foul and painful sore came on those who had the mark of the beast and who worshiped its image" (Rev. 16:2). What can we do to avoid such a situation?

One key is to understand that poverty and injustice never happen in a vacuum. It requires the allegiance of many to the powerful few for oppression to occur. Owning the underlying myths and assumptions that uphold their positions of power is a central task of the power elite. Hence the power of "cult" in Rome's day and in the media today.

Once we understand that our allegiances matter, can we, like the imagery in Revelation, cast a new vision of an empire of which Jesus is the center? Can we live in a way that the one who upholds all, especially the most vulnerable, is made lord of all? Can we live with our allegiance to a New Jerusalem, or do we need Babylon too much?

Myth two: Whose peace?

Around the time Revelation was written, the Emperor Augustus claimed to have initiated "Pax Romana," or the "peace of Rome." The basic idea was that in a world of barbarianism, the Roman Empire provided a haven of protection, stability, and harmony for its citizens. A golden age had been initiated.

John exposes this myth through the imagery of Babylon, beasts, and whores. The law-and-order campaign to bring peace came at a price, and John spares no expense in using the strongest possible language and images available to him. The empire's beasts, Babylon, and whores were not benign benefactors providing peace, but nothing less than cold-blooded murderers. Those who would not worship the image of the beast would be killed (Rev. 13:15).

The overlapping image of Babylon as a prostitute also reveals a murderer: "In you [Babylon] was found the blood of prophets and of saints, and of all who have been slaughtered on earth" (Rev. 18:24; see also 16:6 and 17:6).

The lifestyle of peace for Roman citizens came at a massive cost to those on the margins of the empire. The slaves, those militarily subdued, and any who resisted were killed off or exiled, like John. True peace or *shalom* did not come from such military violence aimed at quieting the margins. Real peace is only possible from the one who upholds and protects them.

Now that the United States is the only "superpower" left, the temptation of empire is very real. Why not be the world's peace force and protect its own citizens' interests at the same time? When we hear a world leader vilifying others with slogans such as "They just hate our freedom" or "The evil-doers are against peace," the book of Revelation has something to say as much to this empire as to ones in the past. Military might, used to kill others or to bring peace, can never be finished. There can be no peace while wealth, power, and the military are concentrated in the hands of a few.

John makes clear where lasting peace comes from. It opens the book of Revelation and is a subtext to the imagery employed. "Grace to you and peace from him who is and who was and who is to come, and from the seven spirits who are before his throne, and from Jesus Christ, the faithful witness, the firstborn of the dead, and the ruler of the kings of the earth" (Rev. 1:4b–5a).

Real peace does not come via military might, but from Jesus, the "faithful witness" to the way the world can be and will be for those who reject peace-at-all-costs assumptions.

Myth three: Whose victory?

Closely related to the myth of Pax Romana is the myth of the goddess Victoria. It was she who endorsed the emperor to conquer those who resisted Rome's peace. This assumption, along with the others we have discussed, created an intricate web of myths that enabled the empire's power mostly to go unchallenged. With the promise of victory assured, why would you resist the inevitable? Why feel the full force of being on the wrong side of the gods?

John is an exception. He challenges this assumption, calling each of the seven churches of Asia to "conquer" (Rev. 2:7, 11, 17, 26; 3:5, 12, 21). The Greek equivalent of the Latin *Victoria* is *Nike*, which is used no less than seventeen times in Revelation. The promise of victory that Rome claims is countered by the promise of ultimate victory by the one who conquered death.

Promises have a power of their own. John Piper, in his book *Future Grace*, argues that "no one sins out of duty. We sin because it holds out some promise of happiness. That promise enslaves us until we believe that God is more to be desired than life itself (Ps. 63:3). This means that the power of sin's promise is broken by the power of God's. All that God promises to be for us in Jesus stands over against that which sin promises to be for us without him" (9–10).

So it's the promise in the assured victory of Jesus that gives his followers the courage and hope to see this victory above all else in every aspect of life. The promise of the empire's victory can never be fulfilled. There will never be peace for all through Rome's violence. Only God's promises can hold firm for all.

John is clear about the rewards promised to the churches that conquer. Each church is offered rewards for victory (Rev. 2–3) that are ultimately realized in the New Jerusalem (Rev. 21–22). An example of this is the church in Sardis, where they are promised to be acknowledged before God the Father and not to have their name blotted out in the book of life (Rev. 3:5). This will be fulfilled when the book of life is opened; those who practiced vices will not be in it, but those "who conquer will inherit these things [the New Jerusalem], and I will be their God and they will be my children" (Rev. 21:7).

Such promises of future glory should inspire us to overcome the power of oppression and injustice today. As God's children, we will inherit more than we could ever imagine if we work with our earthly lives for the New Jerusalem.

This is where there are choices to make. Here we are asked to take a stand. Will we stand against the power elite and its promises to us, or will we have the courage to believe God's promises and stand with the poor against the empire? Those who follow Jesus should seek above all else the victory of his rule. Will we conquer the empire by the blood of the Lamb and by the word of our testimony (Rev. 12:11)?

Myth four: Faith to whom?

In John's time, the Latin *fides* (Greek *pistis*) was understood as loyalty or fidelity to the empire. It was the glue for how the social structure of the patron-client relationship worked. For example, if a conquered people were to survive, they needed to give their *fides* to Caesar. They would not be wiped out if they surrendered all to Rome—Rome would look after them. *Fides* couldn't be divided between patrons. Rome would not take kindly to those who didn't give their full *fides* to them or tried to share it with another power. Patrons could give *fides* only to one lord, or else be "at war." Most English Bibles translate *fides/pistis* as "faith." We often use the word "faith" as a similar word to "trust." However, there's no exclusivity attached to trust— we can trust in all kinds of people, institutions, and powers at the same time. This was not the meaning of *fides* in John's time. For example, Jesus commends the churches in Pergamum (Rev. 2:13) and Thyatira (Rev. 2:19) for their exclusive *pistis*. To Smyrna Jesus warns: "Do not fear what you are about to suffer. Beware, the devil is about to throw some of you into prison so that you may be tested, and for ten days you will have affliction. Be faithful [*pistis*] until death, and I will give you the crown of life" (Rev. 2:10).

Exclusive loyalty to Jesus is brutally tested by an empire that wants its citizens to have exclusive faith in it. Yet, this is not real faith at all (Rev. 21:8). The promise of victory to those who endure and keep the faith, however, is assured by the one who can be trusted to fulfill his promises and obligations—something Rome cannot do. Those who have enduring *pistis* in Jesus are the "holy ones" (Rev. 13:10; 14:12) who receive life.

Myth five: Eternity where?

A final key assumption of the Roman Empire was that it would always last. With the final ushering in of this golden era, things would always be this way. Various gods were believed to have prophesied this. We know that coins from the period were minted with "Aeternitas Populi Romani" ("People of Rome Forever") and with the goddess Aeternitas holding the symbols of eternity—the sun and moon. Indeed, one of Romulus's founding names for Rome was "Urbs Aeterna" or the "Eternal City."

Two thousand years later the myth of Rome's eternal empire looks foolish. Did they really think it would last forever? Yet, in the time of John, this was assumed to be the way things were, and it was encouraged by politics, religion, education, and social standing. The caesars knew that to keep the empire strong they needed to nurture intentionally the assumption that their people's personal investment would not end. If it was to go tomorrow, why would people put up with it?

In this context it is significant that John used the Greek equivalent word *aion* twenty-seven times in Revelation. Indeed, the expression *aionas aionon*, often translated "forever and ever," is used no less than thirteen times. For example, we see that with Jesus there is an eternity for him and his rule: "The kingdom of the world has become the kingdom of our Lord and of his Messiah, and he will reign forever and ever" (Rev. 11:15; see also 1:6; 5:13; 7:12).

This eternal authority flows on to those who join with Jesus. "There will be no more night; they need no light of lamp or sun, for the Lord God will be their light, and they will reign forever and ever" (Rev. 22:5).

Though various economic and political empires may look strong today, this will not always be the case. The only empire that will last is Christ's reign, and we must choose to be part of this above all other empires.

Challenge

Poverty and oppression don't happen in a vacuum. They require sophisticated structures and myths to enable them to continue. They are internalized by poor and non-poor alike as "the way things are." Will we have the courage to face them boldly and honestly? Will we stand against the temporal kingdoms with their myths and stand with the truths the real kingdom offers—truths that will last forever?

Personal Reflection: Battles with Stubborn Poverty

In the process of writing this book, I have experienced two examples of the stubborn nature of poverty in people I care deeply about. The myths of empire have quick solutions for them; I have no response for their despair, but rather only the hope of Christ.

Nom, a neighbor of mine, was recently married and works hard selling clothes at the markets each day. If he makes 100 baht a day ($2.90) profit, it's a good day. Of course, with a rent of 3,000 baht ($90) a month for his one-room shack, there is no way he can let his new bride stop working to start a family. I had an idea to help out. UNOH needed about 200 T-shirts with our conference and benefit CD designs on them. I was running short on time to do this. Nom worked in the industry and knew people who could do this. If Nom organized this for us, we would lend him the capital and sell the T-shirts in Australia for him. If we sold them all within a month, he would make around 90,000 baht ($2,600), or almost three times his annual salary. Seemed like a great deal for all of us!

Though Nom could see it was a great deal and was keen to help us out, he just couldn't do the job. First, he was nervous he would mess it up. Then he lost the number of the guy who could do it. Then he couldn't really take time out of his current job to chase down a quote because his margins were so tight with the wet weather cancelling some market days. Then he became ill for a while. In the end he had to pass, leaving me to chase it down at the last minute. We did this, and the money being made is going back into helping provide no-interest loans for those with small start-up business ideas. I hope that one day Nom will have the confidence and energy to pursue this.

What this story illustrates, however, is that nice, neat "big-picture" formulas in boardrooms don't always translate into the end of poverty at the grassroots. It takes people to love people back to life—life on life, taking poverty personally.

This is not saying efforts like the Millennium Goals, Live 8, and other structural efforts are a waste of time. They are crucial, too. Ridding economies of debt, and having fairer and more just social and trade systems, both give everyone a better opportunity to live as God intends. I suggest, however, that good systems are not enough. There is evil in the world that has not finished its work yet, and people risking themselves to work with people in poverty is a key part of ending poverty as we know it.

Evil preys on the most vulnerable. On hovered over his paper, his pen ready in his tiny hand, huge eyes looking up, eager to pounce on the next question. Many factors make the answers harder to come by for On than most. Not least among these is the fact that he was "thrown out" by his parents, who eventually died of HIV/AIDS, and now lives with his elderly grandma in a plywood shack not much bigger than a single bed, a home due to be demolished. Yet, despite all the odds, On is trying to make the most of what he has in my English class during his school holidays.

If you can read this book, it is likely that significant others joined with you to develop your literacy and numeracy skills. The sad reality for six-year-old On is that if he doesn't learn these skills now at the Klong Toey Community Center, he will most likely not have the opportunity when he enters the public school system next year. Joining classes of over sixty students per teacher means that only the fittest survive, nevermind learning the required life foundations that many of us take for granted. Given On's home life, survival will be his first priority—and second and third—and then maybe somewhere way down the list, the three Rs might get a look in. Almost certainly the temptations to escape the battle with alcohol, glue sniffing, and *ya ba* (methamphetamine) will come knocking on his door sooner than later. "Birds of prey" seem to be circling On's life already.

Yet, despite what has been and what could come, here is a sacred childhood moment for On that can never be taken away from him—a chance to enjoy learning. For over twenty years the Klong Toey Community Center's preschool has been providing such moments: basic literacy, numeracy, and life-skills education for Klong Toey's slum children. By using the Montessori method that individualizes the learning, the Thai staff give On—and literally thousands like him over the years—a chance not to be left behind.

Optimism is impossible, despair is a cop out; all that is left is Christian hope. When all around is creating a grinding despair, perhaps all we have to offer is this Christian hope—that things don't have to be this way. Please pray that On and Nom and the many like them will find this hope and help to make Klong Toey the community God intends—one that keeps doubt, despair, and hate at bay and bubbles over with the enduring qualities of faith, hope, and love.

Perhaps this is part of the meaning of the Bible's strange use of apocalyptic language. There is an assured end that has all evil banished, and all justice done, but in-between times there is a raging war with all kinds of beasts and monsters. The casualties of this war are the world's most vulnerable, towards whom evil targets its powers. Of course, the sting in the tail of this literature is that the end judgment is full of surprises. We could be on the wrong side at the end of the world.

Jesus takes up this theme with a fury and tells the parable of the sheep and the goats. It is worth reading all the way through in Matthew's Gospel, 25:31 to the end of the chapter. "When did we see you hungry . . . thirsty . . . homeless . . . naked . . . sick . . . in prison?" was asked by the many separated from God like goats. "Truly I tell you, just as you did not do it to one of the least of these, you did not do it to me," came Jesus's reply.

This is not about salvation by works, but simply what will have lasting meaning and purpose—that is, what we do and don't do with respect to Jesus. In fact, Jesus tells us our whole lives will be evaluated on the basis of what we do and don't do with him as he is found in the "least of these." Do we experience God's grace enough to act against the myths of our day, or do we cave in to their demands and miss Jesus and his will altogether?

If we died tonight, would a poor person give us a letter of reference for heaven? What would the least of these brothers and sisters say about us? Jesus says that this is the litmus test of whether we have joined Jesus or not in this life. Do anything, but don't miss out on eternal life by making a quick buck on the material treadmill in this life. We are made to change the world, not just change the products we consume.

Questions for Discussion

- What do you want to live on after you have died?
- Can you identify some of the myths about poverty that have fooled you and your faith community?
- Reflect on a myth that you have resisted. What "stereotypes," "sayings," or "wisdom" have you identified as false and been able to take a stand against? What helped or hindered this resistance?
- To provide an alternative to the lies of the empire, we must find support. What kind of support has been helpful for you, and where could you find more?

A Personal Exercise

Take some time to visualize two people and what they would say to you:

- A person you know who is successful in the world's eyes, someone who has lived the myths of the empire with gusto. This empire is now about to be judged by God, and this person is witnessing against you. If they were giving testimony about your collaboration with the falling empire, what would they say?
- A person that you have met who is facing poverty. If that person had to write a letter of reference to Jesus for you, to pardon you, what would they write? Try to write this out as honestly as you can, thinking about this person's voice and life and how you have and have not connected with them.

Our faith is all of grace, but evidence of where our faith lies is found in these two testimonies. Spend some time rewriting these as if you could resist the empire. Receive from both the testimonies what Jesus would want you to have.

- How would they be different or similar?
- What could you ask Jesus for to help make the changes?

Final Challenge
Will We Make Poverty Personal?

Do we believe the Christian faith enough to go wild-eyed and insanely radical about it?

Are we prepared to care about what poverty does to people the way Jesus does? I came across the following quote from Mick Duncan's book, *Who Stands Fast? Discipleship in Difficult Places,* that put a shudder through my spine.

> I lament the death of outrage. Without a sense of outrage we run the serious risk of being ordinary when God created us to be extraordinary. Outrage makes you do things that are out of the ordinary. Without it we run the risk of becoming nice people in a nice church. To be honest, that makes me want to reach for the nearest bucket. That may seem a bit harsh but we do get an echo of this in the Book of Revelation where God vomits over lukewarm believers. God only gave us ten commandments; there is no eleventh that says, "Thou shalt be nice." Jesus, the head of the church, is no Mr. Nice Guy. Christians seem to have bought

into the sickening idea that niceness is the essence of goodness. No more of this insipid niceness. A nice soldier is an oxymoron. Nice soldiers do not win wars.

Duncan, Who Stands Fast?

Our whole family was gearing up to go to Australia again for our "Surrender 05: Decisions for Life" conference as I read this quote the first time. To be honest, just the thought of trying to convey again what happens each day here in Klong Toey to those in Australia was overwhelming. If I could get the average Aussie to have even a little sense of the realities here, it would make us all feel uncomfortable. I really like most people I meet, and I'd prefer just to get along with everyone and not be antisocial. I hate being the guy others want to avoid.

There is another factor here, too, in my impulse to be nice. Rather than being antisocial via outrage, life here can sometimes create a kind of numbness in me. To be exposed to so many sad stories each day can make me immune.

Yet, on the Monday night before I left, I sat with Pastor Suwot and he told of his pain after being kicked out of his home, church, and community building after fifteen years. The outrage Mick talked about began to well up in me.

The fact that it was a Christian foundation doing this to our church made it worse. Where would Ta Rua Church base itself? Where would Suwot and his family live? What could we do? Would Christians in Australia even care with all that goes on there?

Then, as if by a divine hand, I heard a song that helped to make sense of what was going on in me. Rivertribe's Mike Lane, who organized UNOH's first benefit CD, *Surrender: Songs from the Silence*, sent me some MP3s for review. While all sixteen tracks, donated from artists in Australia, the US, and UK, are incredible, it was Welsh singer-songwriter Martyn Joseph who awoke my heart that day. Toward the end of his song Martyn sings:

I woke shaking and thinking about love that's in the
world
And if there is no bigger picture then it's all obscene,
absurd
So you can pass me that revolver there but pass me a
book I've read
Pass me a fresh cut flower, sir, but don't ask me what I
dread
That the good in me is dead.

Please pray we will not experience this "dread"—that the good
in me will not be dead nor the Christlike outrage of too many poor
and oppressed be suppressed by my wanting to be acceptable. I
pray, too, for those who read this book, that it will open you up
to God's outrage expressed in the Bible and inspire you to deep,
responsive actions.

Where Are We Investing Our Lives?

Jesus's parable of the rich fool in Luke 12:13–34 questions where
we invest our best time, energy, and concerns. Perhaps this Bible
text is as good as any to consider as a final challenge in our reflections on the Bible's call to end poverty.

The context leading to this is one of Jesus resisting the power
brokers and the powers. Jesus had just angered the Pharisees and
scholars in their own home by teaching that acceptance by God
comes not from greedy lives that look clean, but generous lives
shared with the poor (Luke 11:39–41); not from tithing, but justice
and love (Luke 11:42); not from status seeking and exclusion, but
serving (Luke 11:43–54). These power brokers were insulted (Luke
11:45) and opposed Jesus fiercely. As Jesus left, a mob of many
thousands gathered, so that "they trampled on one another" (Luke
12:1). Those who have been in a mob situation know that the
fear can be almost tangible. Jesus drew his disciples close at that
point and called them to have courage in the face of the powers

of the Pharisees and scholars. God would have the ultimate say over their lives (Luke 12:2–12).

A voice from someone in the crowd intervened and said, "Teacher, tell my brother to divide the family inheritance with me" (Luke 12:13). The crowd hushed, straining to hear the answer. Yet, Jesus refused to arbitrate over a dead person's possessions and moved rather to address the crowd. He warned them, "Take care! Be on your guard against all kinds of greed; for one's life does not consist in the abundance of possessions" (Luke 12:15). This word "greed" has to do with "desiring more," and Jesus then told the famous parable of a certain rich man who was willing to defer his happiness by building bigger and bigger barns to store his surplus grain, with the idea that one day he could take life easy, eat, drink, and be merry. But he died. God then called him a "fool," asking what he had invested his life in.

Jesus explained the point of the parable, "So it is for those who store up treasures for themselves but are not rich toward God" (Luke 12:21), and shows the folly of letting possessions like clothes, food, buildings, or careers, which are "here today and gone tomorrow," possess us.

We live in a world that does not take these warnings about greed seriously or personally. Just before I was due to fly to Australia for our annual conference, we had a huge storm in Klong Toey, and our TV channels changed around. Suddenly, we had ABC Asia-Pacific TV, and the latest news from Australia came on. There was Australia's treasurer, Peter Costello, out in front of a huge Christian conference in Sydney, being asked a question of faith. "Mr. Costello, do you believe Jesus will make you rich and prosperous?"

"Well," said the treasurer, "it hasn't worked for me." Both men chuckled.

What most struck me as I watched this one-liner from a slum was how one of the most powerful people in one of the richest countries on earth could claim not to be rich or prosperous. This is something of a trend among the rich in the world today, as Clive Hamilton's *Affluenza* outlines. Jon Owen, one of our UNOH workers in Melbourne, had sent me the book to help me prepare for the mood that would await me. I was shocked to read the following: "Sixty-two percent of Australians believe they cannot afford to buy everything they really need. When we consider that Australia is one of the world's richest countries and Australians today have incomes three times higher than in 1950, it is remarkable that so many people feel their incomes are inadequate" (59).

To be honest, I thought Hamilton was exaggerating about Australians "crying poor." Yet, there was Costello on my TV screen. When I did visit Australia, the increasing size of homes really struck me. Each family member seemed to have a room for their own TV and computer, and they lived separate lives. A friend even admitted that their daughter e-mailed him from the next room asking to meet in the kitchen for a coffee!

The bigger houses, cars, and jobs for which people seem to sacrifice everything will not last. One of the saddest illustrations of this in Hamilton's book is a story of a merchant banker who finally gave into his wife's nagging and took a day off work to spend with his teenage son. They spent the day sailing in Sydney harbor and, while it would be the only time they did this, the son was overjoyed. Then the merchant banker died suddenly of a heart attack a few weeks later. After the funeral, the son searched through his father's office diary and looked up the date of their outing. He found only these words, "Wasted day." Jesus's question comes to mind: "For what will it profit them if they gain the whole world but forfeit their life?" (Matt. 16:26) The man had lost all perspective of what mattered and what would live on after he died.

The question we all have to ask is, Where are we really investing our lives? Will we be the tragic figures who invested our best time, energy, and love into things that ended up literally in the trash?

Making Our Lives Count

It doesn't have to be this way. The Gospel story has good news for us. Jesus says, "Strive for [God's] kingdom, and these things will be given to you as well" (Luke 12:31). If we surrender our lives to Christ, we will be given the authority in the kingdom to live as God intends. This grace gives us the world not as a possession, but as an eternal inheritance.

Yet, there is a price to pay for our lives to count. Jesus explained, "Sell your possessions, and give alms" (Luke 12:33a). This is how we receive the inheritance. This is how we get a bigger and better family. We give everything we have to join with Jesus among those facing poverty. On the side of those facing oppression is the authority of God's reign.

Jesus commanded, "Make purses for yourselves that do not wear out, an unfailing treasure in heaven, where no thief comes near and no moth destroys" (Luke 12:33b). Some things do last and count forever: when we love people and really care about what happens to them, we make a deposit on our eternal inheritance. Our acts of mercy and compassion are the only things that will last forever. Everything else will rot away. This is similar to what the apostle Paul wrote in his first letter to the Corinthians. "And now faith, hope, and love abide, these three; and the greatest of these is love" (1 Cor. 13:13).

Jesus explained, "For where your treasure is, there your heart will be also" (Luke 12:34). Our treasure is our best time, energy, and resources. If we do a quick inventory of how we spent the last week, Jesus would say that is what we really care about. To gain the eternal treasure, then, will require us to turn around our lives—repent—towards the poor. This is a conversion of sorts, evidenced by where we put our earthly treasures.

We may not have covered all 2,000 or so Bible verses relating to poverty, neither have we been able to tease out every implication. However, I pray that through this book you have received an orientation, an inspiration to love God and neighbor afresh. John's epistle puts it this way:

> We know love by this, that he laid down his life for us—and we ought to lay down our lives for one another. How does God's love abide in anyone who has the world's goods and sees a brother or

sister in need and yet refuses help? Little children, let us love, not in word or speech, but in truth and action.

1 John 3:16–18

This compassion is not an abstract idea, but a call to take up Jesus's invitation to enter personally into the reality of human mess and suffering. Our planet's future is tied up in this. Will the dreams of *shalom* happen? If each of us will surrender to Jesus, give all we have to the poor, and live a meaningful, compassionate life, we have every chance.

Such a life may seem temporally insane for some, but it has the promise of eternal significance. Perhaps living among the poor is a better place than most for the opportunity for Paul's prayer for the Colossians to be answered:

May [you] be filled with the knowledge of God's will in all spiritual wisdom and understanding, so that you may lead lives worthy of the Lord, fully pleasing to him, as you bear fruit in every good work and as you grow in the knowledge of God.

Colossians 1:9–10

Will we take Jesus and poverty personally? Those who read these kinds of books probably do. The real question is an eternal one of whether we are personally part of the problem of oppressing Jesus and the poor, or part of real solutions in seeing liberation, joining God's reign as it invades our vulnerable world. My prayer for us all is that we would be diligent servants working on the right side of what Jesus takes personally. I pray we can hear Jesus say of each of us, "Well done, good and faithful servant."

Bibliography

Barker, Ash. *Collective Witness: A Theology and Praxis for a Missionary Order*. Springvale, Victoria: UNOH Publications, 2000.

_____. *Finding Life: Reflections from a Bangkok Slum*. Springvale, Victoria: UNOH Publications, 2003.

_____. *Making Connections: Stories, Exercises, and Questions to Help Encounter Christ Today*. Springvale, Victoria: UNOH Publications, 1998.

_____. *Surrender All: A Call to Sub-Merge with Christ*. Springvale, Victoria: UNOH Publications, 2005.

Berger, Peter. *The Sacred Canopy*. New York: Anchor Books, 1990.

Bosch, David J. *Transforming Mission: Paradigm Shifts in Theology of Mission*. Maryknoll, NY: Orbis, 1991.

Brueggemann, Walter. *The Prophetic Imagination*. Minneapolis: Fortress Press, 1978.

Claiborne, Shane. *The Irresistible Revolution: Living as an Ordinary Radical*. Grand Rapids: Zondervan, 2006.

Collins, Jim. *Good to Great: Why Some Companies Make the Leap . . . and Others Don't*. New York: Collins, 2001.

Day, Dorothy. *By Little and by Little: The Selected Writings of Dorothy Day*. Edited by Robert Ellsberg. New York: Alfred A. Knopf, 1983.

De Botton, Alain. *Status Anxiety*. New York: Vintage, 2005.

De Soto, Hernando. *The Mystery of Capital: Why Capitalism Triumphs in the West and Fails Everywhere Else*. New York: Basic Books, 2003.

Dostoyevsky, Fyodor. *The Brothers Karamazov*. Translated by Constance Garnett. New York: Random House, 1996.

Duncan, Mick. *Who Stands Fast? Discipleship in Difficult Places*. Springvale, Victoria: UNOH Publications, 2005.

Greeff, Reiner, and Trevor W. King. *Medicine Man Chief*. Auckland: Tribal Truth, 2002.

Gutiérrez, Gustavo. *A Theology of Liberation*. London: SCM Press, 1974.

Hamilton, Clive. *Affluenza: When Too Much Is Never Enough*. Sydney: Allen & Unwin, 2005.

Hayes, John. *Sub-merge: Living Deep in a Shallow World*. Ventura, CA: Regal Books, 2006.

Heschel, Abraham. *The Prophets*. 2 vols. New York: Harper, 1962.

Houston, Brian. *You Need More Money: Discovering God's Amazing Financial Plan for Your Life.* Colorado Springs: STL, 2000.

Howard-Brook, Wes, and Anthony Gwyther. *Unveiling Empire: Reading Revelation Then and Now*. Maryknoll, NY: Orbis, 1999.

LaHaye,Tim and Jerry B. Jenkins, *Left Behind*. Carol Stream, IL: Tyndale, 1996.

Lewis, C. S. *Reflections on the Psalms*. New York: Harvest Books, 1958.

Lewis, Oscar. *Five Families: Mexican Case Studies in the Culture of Poverty*. New York: Basic Books, 1975.

Lindsey, Hal. *The Late, Great Planet Earth*. Grand Rapids: Zondervan, 1970.

Malinowski, Bronislaw. *Magic, Science, and Religion, and Other Essays*. Westport, CT: Greenwood Press, 1984.

Morgan, Timothy C. "Purpose Driven in Rwanda." *Christianity Today*. October 2005.

Piper, John. *Future Grace*. Colorado Springs: Multnomah, 1995.

Sachs, Jeffrey. *The End of Poverty: Economic Possibilities of Our Time*. New York: Penguin, 2006.

Sobrino, Jon. *The Principle of Mercy: Taking the Crucified People from the Cross*. Maryknoll, NY: Orbis, 1994.

Sider, Ronald J. *Rich Christians in an Age of Hunger*. Dallas: Word, 1997.

Warren, Rick. *The Purpose Driven Life: What on Earth Am I Here For?* Grand Rapids: Zondervan, 2002.

Wright, Christopher. "Leviticus." In *The Bible for Everyday Life*. Edited by George Carey. Grand Rapids: Eerdmans, 1996.

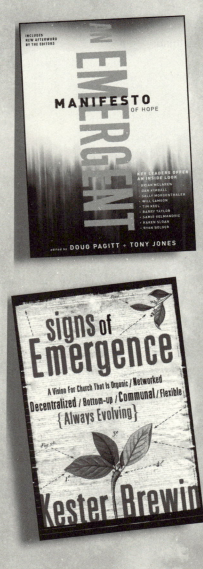
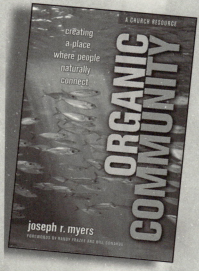

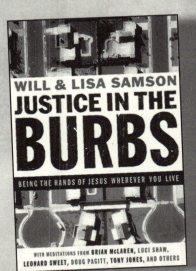

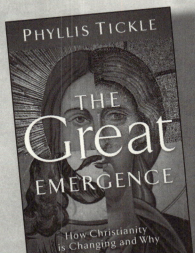
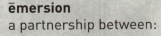